Contents

Editorial

Helen O'Connell

It is timely that in 1993, the year of the United Nations World Conference on Human Rights, a non-governmental organisation, such as Oxfam, should produce a journal on gender and conflict. Situations of conflict pose serious problems for those caught up in them and for agencies working for long-term and equitable development. War and civil strife are widespread and work in conflict situations absorbs a significant and increasing proportion of the resources of local and international non-governmental organisations. There is full-scale war in many countries, for example Angola and the territories of the former Yugoslavia. There is armed conflict in the Philippines, South Africa, Guatemala, Colombia, Sri Lanka, Western Sahara and in many other places. Military force is used systematically in many countries to curb any challenge or opposition.

In situations of war or violent conflict all civilians suffer. However, there are many gender-specific human-rights issues which organisations involved in development, relief, and emergency work need to be aware of and address in their interventions. War creates specific gender-related difficulties for women which are explored in this *Focus on Gender*. Until quite recently, for example, certain kinds of human-rights abuses, those suffered primarily by men — imprisonment, torture, killings — were monitored and publicised by human-rights organisations, while human-rights abuses of women remained largely invisible except to the women themselves. Gender-sensitive research and monitoring, and the work of women's organisations, have publicised this omission. The war in the territories of the former Yugoslavia has brought rape into public view in Europe as a war crime which requires full investigation and retribution.

Women experience conflict and violence in several ways related explicitly to the gender division of rights, roles and responsibilities. Class and ethnic differences overlay this gender-related experience. The violence suffered by the widows in the El Quiché district of Guatemala, described in Judith Zur's article, is inextricably linked to their marginalisation as Indians. Similarly, the impact of the war on women in Chad, Cambodia, and Afghanistan written about in this issue, is exacerbated because these women are from the poorest and most oppressed social groups.

Oxfam has been concerned with issues of gender and conflict for several years, and, amongst other activities, has undertaken a consultation with all its Field Offices, written papers on refugee issues, and provided grants to organisations working with women in war situations.

This year the Gender and Development Unit conducted a workshop on the theme for Oxfam staff and partner organisations in South-East Asia.

This issue of *Focus on Gender* concentrates on gender issues in situations of military and civil strife. It examines the effects of armed conflict on women's lives and the appalling situation in which many women refugees and displaced find themselves. But we felt it was essential to include other aspects of North/South conflict, and conflict between men and women, to reflect more accurately the range of conflict situations which confront women.

In all countries, including those sympathetic to women's equality, women remain second-class citizens. Women suffer daily infringement of their basic rights as human beings, and live with the ever-present threat or experience of physical and sexual violence. The perpetrators of violence are predominantly but not exclusively male; there are many instances of violence by women against other women, for example, by older in-laws against younger, and of violence by women against men. Violence may often come from those from whom one most expects protection: older family members, community elders, state institutions. Violence against women is used to keep women in their place, to limit their opportunities to live, learn, work and care as full human beings, to hamper their capabilities to organise and claim their rights. It is a major obstacle to women's empowerment, and their full participation in shaping the economic, social and political life of their countries.

The departure point in the exploration of conflict in this *Focus* is an analysis of patriarchy as an ideology which fosters discriminatory treatment and sanctions violence as a legitimate instrument to maintain the *status quo*. As is argued clearly in the opening article by Judy El Bushra

In many countries in the South, armed conflict is a part of daily reality. This is Angola, where the war which began in 1975 has not yet ended.   KEITH BERNSTEIN/OXFAM

and Eugenia Piza-Lopez, gender-related violence which 'embodies the imbalances inherent in patriarchal society' takes many forms. It can range from rape, domestic violence and child abuse to military and political violence, torture, and the reduction in state services leading to increased stress and workload for women.

Nelia Sancho-Liao's article also emphasises the extent of gender-related violence and is a powerful indictment of the political, economic and social structures which institutionalise violence against women. She provides incontrovertible evidence of the error of separating social and economic from civil rights. She describes the position of the majority of women in Asia, who as landless peasants, urban street traders, factory workers, prostitutes and migrant domestic workers, are socially and economically on 'the margins of the margins'. For them, human rights must include access to basic resources and respect as human beings.

A number of articles draw attention to the gender-related impact of war on women. Fiona McLachan writes about the trauma and hardship haunting Afghan women because of the war. Achta Djibrine Sy describes the dramatic effects of the 1979-1982 civil war on Chad which tore that country apart and 'forced women into the vanguard of the struggle for survival'. The interview with Sochua Mu Leiper gives a vivid account of the enormous problems facing Cambodian women, now over 60 per cent of the population, following 20 years of war and strife.

Several articles emphasise the psychological and social impact of conflict situations on women. Judith Zur's piece on Guatemala examines the psychological and social impact of government-sponsored terrorism on widows in the El Quiché district of Guatemala. She writes about the fear and insecurity that mark women's lives after years of violence, and the torment caused by not knowing the whereabouts of

a 'disappeared' relative, and not being able to bury the dead. This and other articles draw attention to the fact that psychological disorders frequently manifest themselves as physical ailments. Stigma is attached to mental illness in almost all countries, and misconceptions abound: physical illnesses are socially and culturally acceptable, psychological problems are not.

A number of common themes emerge: women's added vulnerability to rape and sexual abuse in times of conflict; the rapid increase in the numbers of households primarily or exclusively dependent on women's labour to survive, and the consequent excessive burden this places on women's shoulders at a time when they too are experiencing emotional and economic stress; the total disruption of economic and social life and, paradoxically, the opportunities this creates for women to overcome some aspects of the traditional gender division of roles.

The displacement of millions of women, men and children from their homes because of military conflict causes social, economic, and emotional disruption. The UN High Commissioner for Refugees (UNHCR) reports that there are presently around 20 million refugees worldwide who have fled their home countries in the face of persecution; over 80 per cent are women and their dependent children, and elderly people. UNHCR estimates that another 25 million people are displaced within their own countries. Here again, the gender implications were late in receiving attention. The specific needs of women for protection, food, health care, income to provide for their families, and education are now being researched and documen-ted; they are slowly, but not yet compre-hensively, being addressed. Tina Wallace identifies a number of important areas where action is needed, for example, in agencies' staffing and staff training, in research and policy, in the involvement of refugee and displaced women in planning and decision-making.

The opportunities for empowerment and politicisation which may arise for women in situations of conflict are noted by many writers. When men are absent, the full weight of family survival falls on women who are compelled, and enabled, to take on roles from which they may have been excluded in more peaceful times. Although the personal costs to women are high in terms of physical and emotional stress, the gains in confidence, self-worth and powerfulness can be enormous. The challenge is, for women themselves and for NGOs working with them, to ensure these gains survive the conflict times. The process of empowerment, of women's self-education and organisation, needs to begin immediately in conflict situations and receive all available support.

Physical and sexual violence against women does not only occur in times of war. Violence by male partners against women in their own homes, 'domestic violence', occurs across all social groups, races, age-groups, religious and political persuasions. This universality, coupled with women's fear and unwillingness to speak out, explains the silence which has surrounded for so long this violation of women's rights. Recently, largely through the research and campaigns of women's organisations, male violence in the privacy of the home has become an issue for public scrutiny. Northern-based agencies involved in development, wary of allegations of cultural imperialism and mindful, however subconsciously, of the pervasiveness of violence in Northern societies too, have been very reluctant to address 'domestic violence'. Ruth Jacobson's article demonstrates the scale of the problem and argues persuasively why it should be of particular concern to agencies which claim to be committed to improving the lives of men and women in Southern countries.

Forced prostitution is another aspect of the violation of women's human rights. The Anti-Slavery International presentation to the 1992 meeting of the United Nations Working Group on Contemporary Forms of Slavery details how women and minors, enticed by promises of canteen jobs, are forced to work in brothels near mining encampments and large civil construction projects in the north of Brazil. The use of women's bodies to carry drugs is a relatively new form of abuse. Jo Fisher in her piece about Colombian women imprisoned in the UK for drug-carrying offences, shows vividly how poverty, and the fear of violent reprisal can drive women into dangerous situations.

The recognition of women's human rights remains all too easily disregarded in times of crisis.

Violence against the female sex does not start in adulthood. In many societies the female foetus is subject to neglect from the moment of conception; in many the girl child from birth faces subtle or overt discriminatory treatment in terms of access to food, care and education. This subject is raised by many writers in this *Focus* and will be covered more fully in a future issue.

Many writers on gender and development issues, from both South and North, argue cogently that 'development' can constitute a form of violence and generate conflict. This point is raised in the opening article by Judy El Bushra and Eugenia Piza-Lopez. They regard Structural Adjustment Programmes, as 'among the most significant factors in reducing women to poverty and dependence in the Third World'. In their view such programmes have often given rise to increased violence in women's lives and they cite women's 'overwhelming workload' as an aspect of this violence.

Throughout the world, women's organisations and others are working for social and economic change, and much has been achieved. Yet, 45 years since the adoption of the Universal Declaration on Human Rights and 14 years since the adoption of the Convention on the Elimination of All Forms of Discrimination against Women, the recognition of women's human rights remains arbitrary and all too easily disregarded in times of crisis. The four freedoms enshrined in the Universal Declaration on Human Rights and the consequent international human rights covenants: freedom from fear and want, freedom of speech and belief, have never been extended fully to women. The economic and environmental crises of the late twentieth century, coupled with conflict and instability in many countries, jeopardise such progress as women have made towards equality and justice.

Women are not passive victims of situations of struggle and conflict. Women have taken leading roles, including as fighters, in armed conflict on numerous occasions, for example, in Nicaragua against the Contras, in Eritrea in the war for independence from Ethiopia. Women refugees manage daily life in many refugee camps. Women workers in the export-oriented-industrial zones in Sri Lanka, the Philippines, Malaysia and elsewhere have been the first to protest at the exploitative practices of employers. Women, from Scotland to Hong Kong, have organised, often in the teeth of extreme opposition, to protect their jobs and their rights as workers. Unarmed women are in the front line also in anti-apartheid struggles in South Africa and have shown themselves fearless in the face of all forms of aggression. Women have been, and are, in the forefront, too, of working for change, for peace, security and equitable gender relations — essential to the reduction of conflict at all levels and lasting respect for human rights.

Eritrean women training as fighters. Although wars are mainly waged by men, there are some women who take part in armed conflict.   MIKE GOLDWATER/NETWORK

Gender-related violence:

its scope and relevance

Judy El-Bushra and Eugenia Piza Lopez

Prepared for presentation by the National Alliance of Women's Organisations (NAWO) to the NAWO Overseas Development Administration Liaison Group meeting, 29 October 1992 .

The purpose of this paper is to sketch out the parameters of this broad and complex subject, and to identify policy issues for further consideration.

Violence — which we can define as an assault on a person's physical and mental integrity — is an underlying feature of all societies, an undercurrent running through social interaction at many different levels. How a society chooses to control the violence inherent in it reflects the value it places on mutual respect and tolerance of difference, and on human rights, democracy and good governance. Though some countries may have more successful records than others in this respect, gender violence is a worldwide and ever-present phenomenon against which eternal vigilance is necessary.

Gender-related violence, the concern of this paper, is defined as violence which embodies the power imbalances inherent in patriarchal society. Though it is not necessarily carried out by men against women, this is overwhelmingly the form it takes. (Male rape, and some instances of violence by women against other women, such as female genital mutilation, footbinding and the dispossession of widows, should also be seen as gender violence since they reflect aspects of patriarchal domination.) Gender violence takes many forms, of which the following is a tentative list:

- rape, including marital rape and rape as a tool of repression against particular classes or groups
- domestic violence
- child abuse
- female foeticide and infanticide, denial of health care and nutrition for girl children
- sexual and emotional harassment
- genital mutilation
- prostitution
- pornography
- population control, enforced sterilisation
- war and state violence
- exploitation of refugees
- political violence, including that directed at the families of political targets
- reduction in state services leading to increased stress and workload for women.

Further categorisation is difficult since there are underlying causative factors cutting across all these manifestations of violence. However, we can identify three levels at which violence may touch women's lives: personal, household, and public.

Personal violence

Women experience personal violence as both a physical and a mental affront. The physical toll is enormous, though not yet adequately documented. Some random examples: in the United States, battery from husbands and partners is the leading cause of injury to adult women; in Peru, 70 per cent of all reported crime involves women beaten by their partners; in Mexico 95 per cent of women workers experience sexual harassment from colleagues at work; in Delhi an average of two women per day were burned alive in dowry-related incidents during 1983; the World Health Organisation estimates that more than 90 million African women and girls are victims of genital mutilation. Violence affects women also in terms of their mental health, by sapping their self-esteem and self-confidence, limiting their capacity to solve their own problems, as well as their capacity to develop relationships with others.

Gender violence, and the threat of it, reflect culturally-defined notions of masculinity and femininity which serve to reinforce women's subordinate position. Male and female children are socialised into an acceptance of gender violence; it is an integral part of gender identity. Women learn from an early age that their behaviour may provoke violence from men and they modify their behaviour accordingly. In this way they may be effectively building the walls of their own prison. People who suffer violence may themselves take their frustrations out on others whom they perceive as more vulnerable than themselves (such as younger siblings or daughters-in-law). However, since both male violence and women's acceptance of it are learned, they can also be unlearned.

Violence within the household

Although the family may provide its members with both a physical and a psychological haven, it is paradoxically also true that power imbalances within and between households can lead to suffering and abuse. Forms of gender violence existing at this level, which are often sanctioned by prevailing codes of conduct, include rape, wife-beating, female genital mutilation, attacks on divorced women (viewed as 'fair game'), and child abuse. Worldwide, a high proportion of incidences of violence against women — between 10 and 80 per cent according to various estimates — take place in the home, making the home one of the most dangerous places for women. Discrimination against women operating at this level includes discrimination against girls in access to health and education, the operation of dual standards in evaluating the conduct of boys and girls, early and forced marriage for girls, exchange marriage, exclusion of female household members from participation in decision making, and exclusion of widows from the extended family. Such manifestations of discrimination foster an environment in which physical and mental abuse of women is seen as acceptable, even proper.

Public violence

At the public level there is both culturally sanctioned violence and discrimination (social attitudes to rape, for example, or the relatively lenient sentences meted out in courts to male perpetrators) and the violence which results from the oppression of the state or powerful elements within it. The latter has been given more attention internationally than less visible manifestations of gender violence, having been discussed in connection with human rights issues, legal reforms, and international conventions. To a small but increasing degree its profile has been raised by campaigns by women's groups and organisations dealing with civil liberties and political rights. However, the issues at the public level are wider than this. Every government or authority structure has the

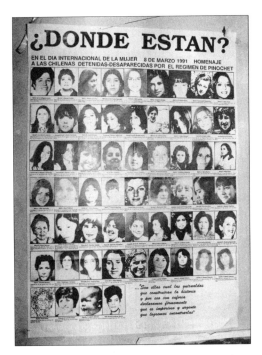

Argentina. Poster showing the faces of women who were among the 'disappeared'
MARIAN POCOCK/OXFAM

power to introduce and uphold measures which guarantee women's rights in a wide range of areas, including rights to land and other property, inheritance, employment and access to services, family law, and so on. Such measures are not only positive in themselves but also foster positive public perceptions of women's rights and dignity.

An issue to be addressed at the public level is the apparent difference from one society to another in the degree of tolerance of male violence. National leaders and those in authority have considerable power to influence attitudes on the acceptability of aggressive or abusive behaviour; at the same time, societies that are themselves under pressure or in the process of disintegration appear to be particularly prone to victimising their more vulnerable members. It is not clear at present what factors may contribute to such differences between societies.

In summary, violence against women is not merely a matter of private relationships, nor simply a question of isolated aberrations that can be brought under public control. It is a wide-ranging and complex question, the manifestations of which have not yet been adequately documented, and which needs to be addressed at a number of different levels. It is, however, beyond the scope of this paper to pursue the full extent of the issue.

Development which abuses women

Development policies and programmes have been among the most significant factors in reducing women to poverty and dependence in the Third World. Well-documented examples show how women have actually been left dispossessed and disenfranchised by development projects which ignore their needs, knowledge and rights. (The Jahaly-Pacharr project in the Gambia, which turned many independent women rice-farmers into agricultural labourers, is the classic example.) The prevailing development model, with its stress on economic growth through technology as the main criterion for development, sidesteps the requirement for empowerment and human growth and hence cannot form an adequate policy framework for a gender-equitable approach.

Structural adjustment programmes, which have devolved the full burden of caring for the family on to the household and particularly on to women, must be seen in this context. Such policies increase women's responsibilities and workload and impose ever-increasing constraints to their moving out of poverty.

It is small wonder that development policies and projects have often given rise to increased violence in women's lives. Women's overwhelming workload is an aspect of this violence. In many areas, women's working day begins at dawn and continues without respite until late at night, while it is rare for men to enjoy no rest or leisure during the course of the day. Despite increased awareness of the problem on the part of development planners, many projects still depend for their success on women taking on extra work. Projects designed to introduce labour-saving and production-enhancing technologies may increase women's workload, while bringing them no compensatory benefits. For example, in agricultural systems where women are responsible for routine field operations, the introduction of animal traction as a means of increasing the acreage under cultivation provides men with increased output, while it brings women nothing but extra work burdens. Planners routinely ignore the impact on women of 'improved' technologies.

The impact of violence on women's mental health is hard to overestimate.

Development projects themselves may unwittingly exacerbate tendencies towards violence, by introducing into the community a resource for which people compete. Women are likely to be particularly vulnerable. Examples can be quoted of women farmers being attacked physically by those wishing to appropriate their land or their harvests. In projects where women are openly prioritised as beneficiaries, men may at first acquiesce and then later appropriate the benefits for themselves. Projects which encourage women to gain confidence or to participate in decision making run the risk of provoking violent reprisals against them. Without serious efforts being made to consult women (and men) in the design of projects, sensitive monitoring and follow-up, and a holistic understanding of the problems women face, projects can unintentionally lead

women into physical danger.

The prevailing attitude among development planners is paralleled by some governments who turn a blind eye to large-scale prostitution and sex tourism because it provides a large slice of the national income. Similarly, trafficking in child brides, commercialised marriage arrangements, and other forms of indentured or slave labour are widespread, tolerated because they serve the interests of powerful and wealthy elites.

Areas of policy which appear well-intentioned may be detrimental to women. For example, in some cases the 'Women in Development' (WID) approach has tended to focus on women in isolation, rather than addressing the causes of their subordination; this may result in little more than additional demands being placed on women's time and workload. Another potentially negative policy area is population control initiatives which see women as targets of contraceptive services and supplies rather than independent decision-makers with rights to control their own fertility.

Violence against women as a barrier to sustainable development

Sustainable development requires the full participation of all citizens in the economy, in democratisation processes, and in the protection of the environment. Tendencies which foster violence against women limit their ability to perform the roles required of them in both the private and the public spheres.

The impact of violence on women's mental health is hard to overestimate. Violence erodes their self-esteem, and confidence to work at lifting themselves out of poverty. Social sanctions often prevent women from discussing violence openly; by 'bottling it up' they compound their emotional problems, as well as cutting themselves off from potential sources of support. (Recent cases in the UK have highlighted the long-term effects, which can often remain suppressed for years, of routine violence on women.) The need for support and counselling is particularly acute in disaster and refugee situations, since here women are particularly vulnerable to rape and other forms of sexual violence.

Fear of violence limits women's ability to perform their roles in many ways. Participation in development projects may be limited because women fear reprisals from their husbands. This fear may also limit their ability to participate in organised groups, and confine them to their home instead of working outside the domestic sphere or pursuing other responsibilities. In the United States a survey in 1988 found that 50 per cent of women missed an average of three days' work each month because of domestic violence. Violence limits women's capacity to care for their children; in parts of Mozambique, for example, where a crying child is regarded as a legitimate cause for a husband to beat his wife, many women sedate their children to keep them quiet. Prioritising the needs of violent fathers and husbands over those of other family members may lead to major problems in terms of child nutrition and may be linked, directly or indirectly, with much broader problems of development such as food security and environmental protection.

These consequences of violence represent a staggering waste of human energy and capacity. The cost of dealing with violence against women, even if measured only in terms of direct costs such as medical and psychiatric services, is equally enormous and must far outweigh the cost of initiatives to contain it. For example, the United States Surgeon General reported in 1989 that battered women are four to five times more likely to seek psychiatric care than non-battered

women. He went on to describe violence against women as 'an overwhelming moral, economic and public health burden that our society can no longer bear'. The phenomenon is relatively well-documented in the United States but there is no reason to imagine that similar conclusions might not apply in any other country.

Fear of violence limits women's ability to perform their roles in many ways.

Violence against women is a serious aggravating factor in the spread of AIDS. Women who have been raped run high risks of HIV infection; in some parts of Uganda, for example, especially where there are still concentrations of armed men, counselling agencies are increasingly having to confront the problems of women who have or may have contracted the virus as a result of rape. Many of these women have no alternative subsequently but to turn to prostitution or 'camp-following'. The socio-economic vulnerability of women renders them generally weak in matters of sexual negotiation. A particularly deplorable development in Uganda is the recent habit of some men who, having learnt of the importance of 'safe sex', seek out young girls as sexual partners on the grounds that they cannot possibly be HIV carriers.

Violence against women as a human rights issue

Women suffer human rights abuses both in their own right and by association with their menfolk. At the level of the state, abuses may be directed both at individuals (attacks on political opponents and their families, abuse of women in state custody, and so on) and at groups. Rape in particular may be used as a systematic means of torture, as well as a means of repressing the women concerned and of humiliating their families and indeed whole communities or classes. Uganda, Burma and Bosnia are both fairly recent examples of conflict arenas in which rape has been perpetrated on a large and systematic scale by state militia.

The capacity of the state to promote basic personal rights is also important. Georgina Ashworth (1992) maintains that women have only an 'indirect' relationship with the state, that is, one that is channelled through their fathers or husbands; she goes on to describe how under Western models (exported globally during colonialism), state institutions tend to reinforce men's control over women's sexuality and fertility, their time, work, leisure and movement outside the home, their property and inheritance, without legal retribution. Thus the issue of women's civil rights must not be confined to their political freedoms or to abuses by agents of the state, but must also include the influence of state institutions on gender relations in the personal domain.

Women's rights in international law have only recently begun to attract attention, and a number of important legal instruments do not address women's needs specifically. For example, gender perse-cution has not yet become internationally recognised as legitimate grounds for asylum. The United Nations Expert Group Meeting on Violence against Women recommended in 1991 the adoption of a protocol on gender violence to the Convention on the Elimination of All Forms of Discrimination against Women, which would commit states to recognising the scale and pervasiveness of the problem and to taking action to eradicate it.

In similar vein, the state has a responsibility to take action against cultural norms and customary laws which conflict with basic human rights. Discrepancies between customary and constitutional law exist in most countries and the former tend

to be highly discriminatory against women. Governments tend to have little interest and few resources for combating this situation. Even where constitutional law provides for women's rights, knowledge of these rights is often restricted. Legal education — for both men and women, for individuals and for institutions — is a major priority in order to provide women with an awareness of their rights, and to establish positive norms of behaviour and attitude on the part of men.

Women in war and other crises

Research on aid planning in emergency situations has shown that a community's ability to survive disasters depends on the extent to which it has minimised 'vulner-abilities' and maximised 'capacities'. Strengthening women's status and capacities contributes to the community's ability to withstand the effect of disasters. The importance of women's role in war and other crises is generally overlooked in relief and rehabilitation projects. The potential effectiveness of women as managers of relief projects and supplies is rarely incorporated into emergency planning. Not only do relief and emergency projects frequently undermine women's crisis-management role, but also their potential contribution in post-emergency stages is often ignored, reducing them to permanent dependency on food aid.

Though wars may be mostly fought by men, women are of course deeply affected by war in a number of ways. One of the first effects of war may be the displacement of civilians, leading to the disintegration of communities, the breakdown of mutual support mechanisms, and to reduced access to food and shelter. Such disruption places extraordinary stress on women as family carers and providers, and on their critical roles in maintaining the social fabric

In May, 1992, about 60,000 Rohingya people were living in makeshift shelters, of plastic sheets and branches, on the Bangladesh/Burmese border. They are a minority Muslim group, subject to harassment by the military in Burma. There are reports of women being raped by soldiers, after their menfolk have been forcibly taken away to serve as army porters. HOWARD DAVIES/OXFAM

and in managing food deficits. Other ways in which women may be affected include heightened general levels of personal violence and increased risk of rape.

The extreme example of the impact of war is seen in the situation of refugee communities. Figures from the United Nations High Commissioner for Refugees show that women and children made up around 85 per cent of the 20 million refugees in the world in 1991. Whether they flee as whole communities or as individuals, flight makes refugees vulnerable to attack both from the aggressors from whom they are fleeing and from those at whose mercy they place themselves. Women refugees are particularly vulnerable to rape and sexual harassment as social control breaks down, in addition to the problems they face of resource loss, cultural dislocation, and

psychological trauma.

In post-war situations, the reintegration of (mostly male) ex-combatants into society gives rise to problems of self-esteem and sense of responsibility for men, who may take out their problems on their women-folk. Uganda and Namibia are both countries which have recently been ravaged by war and where problems of readjustment in gender relations have been noted. Though tendencies towards violence exist in all societies, it appears that in those which have experienced deeply traumatising events (such as war, famine, political oppression and drought) a dislocation of the social fabric occurs which gives rise to irreparable social divisions, to an inability to maintain social cohesion and unity, and to multifarious abuses at the level of personal interaction. The impact of such crises on the quality of interpersonal and communal relations is perhaps a potential area for future research.

Despite all this, war and other sorts of crises may have some positive aspects for women. In extending their roles to cover those of absent males, women may discover new capabilities which neither they nor their menfolk thought they had. Communities may be jarred by crisis into a realisation that women's contribution is vital and deserves to be more highly valued. Women themselves may be critically involved in initiatives to end violence and repair intercommunal relations.

Conclusion

In summary, gender violence involves an enormous amount of human suffering and injustice, and encompasses every country and all types and classes of people. Far from characterising regrettable but isolated incidents in the personal domain, violence — or at least potential violence — conditions every woman's life and dominates the lives of millions of women, impeding both their personal development and the contribution they can make to the lives of those around them. We have seen how violence is a complex issue which needs to be analysed in relation to a web of psychological, social, economic and political factors. We have further seen how development initiatives at many levels have been constrained by and contributed to problems resulting from gender violence.

Gender-related violence is a complex and far-reaching issue but one which lies at the heart of current debates about sustainable development, good governance, and quality of life. Addressing gender violence in all these contexts is an important contribution to the pursuit of the Overseas Development Administration's mission statement and primary objectives, especially those concerning good govern-

ment, the reduction of poverty, the promotion of human development (including education, health and the bearing of 'children by choice'), tackling environmental problems, and the improvement of disaster responsiveness.

Combating gender violence requires many specific measures in a varied range of fields, but essentially involves giving increased priority to equalising the well-being and status of men and women across all spheres of development activity. The only lasting solution is to reduce women's political and economic vulnerability, raising their social status and strengthening their ability to gain control over their own lives.

Recommendations for bilateral development cooperation policy

Bilateral development cooperation agencies should take action in the following areas:

Action on international legal instruments

- Promote the Draft Declaration on Violence Against Women.
- Ensure that gender violence is an agenda item in all human rights fora.
- Promote the adoption of gender-related violence and persecution as grounds for asylum in refugee conventions.

Government-to-government institution building and policy support

- Seek ways of assisting governments in receipt of bilateral aid to improve the capacity of state institutions to cope with rape and domestic violence, for example, by training professionals in the police force and social services, promoting the establishment of women's police stations, introducing measures to provide protection for women refugees, assisting in constitutional reform and legal training for state bodies.

- Seek to influence governments in the formulation of population policies, and the provision of family-planning services which do not abuse women's reproductive rights.

Monitoring and evaluation of development and emergency projects

- Introduce gender violence as a specific monitoring point at all stages of the project cycle (including design, implementation and follow-up).
- Assess critically the gender impact of relief and rehabilitation projects and the involvement of women in these projects.

Support to women's organisations and centres working on gender violence

- Make resources available to support and strengthen women's groups working on solidarity, self-help, population issues, legal education and assistance, and human rights; offer training to such groups in organisation and management; and promote and support networking and exchanges between them.
- Build the capacity of documentation and research centres working on issues of gender violence and promote the widest possible circulation of information on the subject.

References and further reading

Ashworth G (1992) 'Women and human rights', (Background Paper for the OECD Devalopment Assistance Committee Expert Group on Women in Development), London, Change.

Bunch C (1991) *Women's Rights as Human Rights: Toward a Re-vision of Human Rights*, New York, Center for Women's Global Leadership.

Carrillo R (1991) *Violence Against Women: An Obstacle to Development*, New York, Center for Women's Global Leadership.

MATCH International Centre (1990) *Linking Women's Global Struggles to End Violence*, Ontario, Canada.

Welsh Women's Aid (1998) *Worldwide Action on Violence Against Women: Report of the International Women's Aid Conference in Cardiff, 1988.*

International Women's Tribune Centre (1991) 'Violence against women: confronting invisible barriers to development', in *The Tribune Newsletter* 46, June.

IsisWICCE (1990/91) 'Poverty and prostitution: a call for international action', *Isis Women's World* 24, Winter.

Foreign and Commonwealth Office (1992) *Annual Report*, London.

Carney J A (1992) *Contract farming and female rice growers in the Gambia, Overseas Development Institute Irrigation Management Network Paper* 15, London.

Anderson M and Woodrow P (1989) *Rising from the ashes: development strategies in times of crisis*, Boulder, Colorado, UNESCOWestview Press.

Judy El Bushra has been Gender Officer since 1988 at ACORD, a consortium of NGOs supporting development programmes in Africa. She is particularly interested in the issues of gender and conflict. She worked in Sudan for six years from 1978 to 1984.

Eugenia Piza-Lopez is co-ordinator of Oxfam's Gender and Development Unit and Gender Adviser for Asia and Latin America. Her previous experience was as a researcher on images of the Third World in the UK, and work on popular education with Central American women. In Costa Rica, where she was born, she was involved in a participatory research project with the University of Costa Rica, and produced films on development issues.

Conflict and the women of Chad

Achta Djibrine Sy *(Translated by Bridget Walker)*

Throughout the world, wars, whether within the same country or between neighbouring countries, lead to the dislocation and disarray of populations. National and international conflicts have terrible repercussions for different social groups. While every family experiences these conflict situations, the most disadvantaged families are further marginalised. Different analyses of the condition of populations experiencing conflict conclude that women and children are the most affected. The case of Chad is one example.

Chad is a vast country comprising three types of landscape: the Sahara to the north, the Sahel at the centre, and the Sudan region to the south. In each region there is a different way of life, economic activity, and culture. The north and centre are Arab Muslim by culture and the people are largely nomadic pastoralists; whereas the south is Animist and Christian and the people are settled farmers. These contrasts are part of the circumstances at the roots of the long war which has lasted for more than two decades. We are talking, therefore of a war provoked by psychological

Commissaire, sub–Prefect and military officer watching an Independence Day parade in Chad in 1985.

difference. But these differences pale into insignificance in comparison to the profound change which has taken place in the situation of women all over the country.

It was the great civil war of 1979 that tore the country apart. The year 1979 is significant because it marks the start of an unforgettable event burned into the memories of every family in Chad. It tore apart the social fabric, broke up families, and forced women into the vanguard of the struggle for survival. It particularly affected women — married, divorced, single and widows — in the large urban areas where the administrative, commercial and economic activities were concentrated.

Position of women before the conflict

The conflict struck at the heart of Chadian society, caused a rupture in social structures and created new tensions. Before 1979, Chadian society was patriarchal. The man alone was recognised as the head of the household. The man was regarded as the sole producer and therefore had to provide for the family. The woman was the recipient. There was one decision maker: the man gave orders, the woman carried them out. All the household goods belonged to the man. This was the context in which children were socialised and educated.

The woman's role was that of biological and social reproduction. Giving birth was the only role which conferred status on women and this status was reinforced by large numbers of children. Every action and every movement made by a woman was done under the authority and control of a man. Certain women, particularly Muslim women, lived in seclusion. A wife who went out during the day, or engaged in commercial activity, would attract the mockery of both family and friends as she would be exposing her husband's inability to meet her needs. Only widows, divorced women, and women married to very poor husbands could challenge these social constraints by engaging in income-earning activities.

The position of women during the conflict

The conditions of life changed in the period of the civil war, 1979 to 1982. Many men went into exile in the Central African Republic, Cameroon, the Congo, Libya, the Ivory Coast and elsewhere, sometimes abandoning their wives and children. Other men remained but were unable to earn money, since the state ceased to function and many other activities were suspended; the majority of men were state employees or worked in the private and informal sectors. Some had difficulty adapting while others started to fish, hunt and work the land. Women were fortunate if their husbands were still alive even if the men were away from home or unable to make a financial contribution.

Social disorder changed gender relations. Women invented and developed new ways of making money in order to enable their families to survive. These survival strategies were as varied as the social position of the women concerned. The poorest women sold their labour: they became maids in the houses of richer families or went from door to door offering to pound grain. Women who were better-off sold their possessions to get working capital: they sold their jewellery, cooking utensils, bedding and clothes.

Whether they remained in the capital city, went back to the village, took refuge in Kousseri (in Cameroon), or on the outskirts of the capital, women all discovered sources of income. Some produced shea nuts, groundnut oil, *dwede* (the local spaghetti), or doughnuts. Others produced alcoholic drinks made from millet or sorghum, such as *bili bili*, *cochat* and *corde*, or a drink distilled from cassava, called *argui*. Yet others cooked and sold food, or

Selling spices in the market at Am Timam, Chad, 1985.   JEREMY HARTLEY/OXFAM

bought and resold products like condiments or fresh, dried or smoked fish.

In addition to petty trading, many women started agricultural and market-gardening enterprises. Others learned dressmaking, embroidery, knitting, or hairdressing while some learned how to organise the sale of drinks at home and in clubs. Some women joined the army. Others turned to prostitution.

Faced with the increasing needs of their families, women had to trade over long distances both inside and outside the country, buying and selling grain, beans, groundnuts, squash, sesame, wrappers, cloth and Gala beer (beer produced by the national brewery). Women defied danger, fatigue and all other constraints to bring in and increase income. Opportunities to make money were very limited; for example, women did not take up activities requiring new technology. Instead, they generally chose food processing by which,

thanks to their domestic skills and expertise, they were able to provide for their families.

Women also created and developed commercial and banking systems amongst themselves. Problems of purchasing and marketing were resolved by relationships and networks created between the women from a region with a surplus of a particular product trading with those in a needy region. As there was no access to banking institutions, women developed a system of *tontines*, a compulsory saving system established by groups of women who each agree to put in a certain sum of money for a given period. The total is then paid out to the members of the group in rotation. The security of the money was assured: the money collected allowed women to improve their business and reinvest significantly, as well as improving the material conditions of their lives.

In conclusion, it is possible to see that the conflict enabled women to leave their private sphere and take part extensively in the public domain. Although the conflict has increased the numbers of women living in poverty and has exhausted women physically, financially, and psychologically, it has been the foundation of an awareness by women of their essential role in the survival of their families and communities.

Women are no longer regarded as consumers but also as producers. The war helped them to break with their traditional submission, to acquire more autonomy and personal self-confidence. The perception of marriage and children has changed too: children are no longer seen as the only guarantee of life for women or the survival of the household. Today, women's role as producers receives, and reinforces, consideration both from their husbands and from Chadian society as a whole.

Achta Djibrine Sy is Oxfam's Women's Project Officer in Chad.

Life during wartime: women and conflict in Afghanistan

Fiona McLachlan

There is no life in Afghanistan. Everyone has died. Even in 100 years I could not regain the life I had before.

Boobshina is a widow, displaced from her home village, now living in a small, damp, mud house in Kabul with her three children. She cannot afford to buy fuel and so does not cook. Her neighbours help her when they can. Yet Boobshina's statement given above refers not to her poverty but to the mental trauma she has suffered during Afghanistan's 14-year civil war.

The interview with Boobshina was part of a three-month study on the impact of the civil war on Afghan women's lives. Growing insecurity in Kabul cut short the study; 40 women were interviewed, the sample was biased towards poor women in Kabul, but included some refugees in Pakistan. The study aimed to elicit women's attitudes and experiences. This approach resulted in women revealing the more intangible aspects of their lives during wartime.

One of the study's main findings was the high incidence of psychosomatic disorders among the women since the war. All complained of headaches; some had them permanently. Other symptoms the women cited were worry, premature ageing, inability to concentrate, inexplicable aches and pains, fainting and temporary paralysis. The study did not have time to consider sensitive topics such as rape and other traumatic incidents. Nevertheless, the extensiveness of the general psychosomatic disorders is serious. 'The kind of pain we have, you can not really explain. We do not feel well. We ask God, if life is so bad then why have you created us?' explained the widow Samaha and her sister, Obeda. But to try and distinguish between the material and emotional causes of mental ill-health would be difficult if not misguided.

Among the women interviewed trauma was predominantly associated with the loss of relatives through death, disappearance or imprisonment. 'I've been losing close relatives one by one... You can stand hunger and thirst, but losing people, that you can't stand', said Samaha. Although the concept of martyrdom gave death a meaning that made grief easier to bear, there were limits to this solace. Some women's grief was so great that they had attempted suicide. 'I no longer want to be alive', said Safura, a widow living with her father. One brother was killed and two disabled because of the war, which 'killed my mother with grief'. All three of Mastourah's sons had fought in the army; two were killed and one was missing. 'Until I die and am buried beside my sons, I cannot forget. If a chicken dies it is hard to forget it, so how can you forget a child?' With the news of the third son's death, she had attempted suicide by throwing herself out of a first-floor window.

Many women became heads of household following the loss of menfolk. This often brought new economic demands and hardship. Although many women found ways of coping, they continued to feel overwhelmed and worried about the future. As Bibifatma said, 'When my husband was killed I forgot about caring for myself. Now I think only of my children.' She had just lost the job she had had for two months, cleaning dried fruit in a factory, and did not know where to begin to look for more work.

Women talked of the loss of the 'good life'. Although this might be a romanticisation of their past, the women constantly linked the destruction of houses, land and livestock with the loss of a sense of home and social order. For many women the changes in their mental health meant that they no longer attended social occasions, or no longer enjoyed them. Mariam is a widow with four young boys. She does not have women to her house any more because: 'I am ashamed of its poverty (and anyway)... Afghanistan is too angry to trust people.' She locks her boys in the house everyday while she is out at work.

Weddings used to be social occasions which women valued and enjoyed. Now many women found that even if they attended weddings, they no longer felt like celebrating. The refugee women in Quetta, Pakistan, said they sometimes cry at weddings, remembering those people who have died. Fariida, displaced in Kabul for 12 years, said, 'Now we sing songs about revolution, fighting and war as these are the only things that we know.' Shamahana, a widow with four children said, 'Now I go to weddings mainly for the children's sake. Since becoming a widow, I get headaches for three days afterwards so I do not like weddings any more.'

Amid the general despair women felt about their lives, children were seen as the great hope for the future. Bibishiriin had seen her son only once or twice in nine years. He, like thousands of Afghan children, had been sent to study in the

Bibi Tula and her surviving children, back in Afghanistan after years as a refugee in Pakistan.
DIANNA MELROSE/OXFAM

former Soviet Union. Now he is 18 years old and beginning a six-year medical degree. Bibishiriin had not heard from him for four months and this was causing her great suffering.

The widespread incidence of psychosomatic disorders caused by grief and poverty represent a serious health problem among Afghan women, and recovery will take time. However, the women were keen to talk about the impact of the war, and one positive outcome of the study was the forum it provided for such discussions.

The study concluded that the emotional and material consequences of the war are inextricably bound up together, for the women of Afghanistan. Agencies working with women in the rehabilitation process should therefore consider programmes that address the issues of emotional trauma and poverty together.

Fiona McLachlan studied anthropology. She has lived in Sudan and Afghanistan and is particularly interested in the problems of refugee women

Working on gender in conflict situations:
some ideas on strategy

Judy El Bushra and Eugenia Piza-Lopez

In developing strategies for effective gender work in conflict situations, agencies must give attention to the question of how they can build relationships with local non-governmental organisations (NGOs) which will enable gender to be addressed jointly in a constructive way. This is a necessity in all circumstances, but in conflict situations additional questions need to be addressed, and a number of additional sensitivities may be present which require confidence and skill on the part of agency staff. Above all, the special dynamics of armed conflict place particular difficulties in the way of agencies which are drawn into an emergency situation only at the moment of conflict. Building constructive relationships with local NGOs demands that the agency establishes a credible profile which can normally only be developed through a long period of collaboration.

In critical circumstances it is all too easy to see the needs of gender equity as being secondary to other goals, such as the political viability or even the survival of the community in the face of oppression or disaster. Important as these are, the community will be constrained in meeting these goals if over half the population is living under impossible burdens. Thus overarching social goals and goals of gender equity should not be seen as either-or alternatives, but as part and parcel of the same search for emancipation. However, to enable local NGOs to move forward in such circumstances, agencies need to raise their own awareness and skills in dealing with gender issues.

Raising gender issues with local NGOs can either strengthen or weaken working relationships: it can strengthen them if it is done as part of a long-term strategy of permanent dialogue; it can weaken them if done on an *ad hoc* basis, which can lead to issues of imperialism and cultural inappropriateness being raised.

A long-term strategy for working with local NGOs should be characterised by open dialogue, the ability to listen to critical questions from partners, transparency in approaches to work, recognition that learning is a two-way process, sufficient time and resources, and clear prioritisation on where to start, who to start with, and why.

In relations with local NGOs, an agency's aim should be to focus on identifying blockages, which should be dealt with in a constructive and collaborative way. Options for working on gender and empowerment in response to conflict depend on the opportunities available at the moment of the response; agencies must be culturally sensitive and avoid preconceived notions of what gender and empowerment does or does not mean in a particular environment. Agencies must recognise, too, that partners face significant practical problems in discussing and dealing with these issues, and provide assistance that takes this into account.

Possible components for a strategy for working with local NGOs on gender and conflict include:

- Joint training workshops on gender and conflict.
- Strengthening ties with and under-standing of women's organisations and movements who have information and insights about the situation of women in the country.
- Strengthening and developing a consistent strategy for networking and information exchange between those working on gender issues and those working on development issues in general.
- Commissioning research which documents and synthesises the experiences of men and women in conflict situations; contracting local and regional researchers for this task and investing resources in documentation and communication of the research findings.
- Strengthening the agency's resource-base of local women consultants, trainers, and experts for employment in conflict situations, which will enhance the likelihood of culturally-sensitive, gender-balanced perspectives being incorporated into planning.
- Prioritising the integration of gender into technical issues in conflict situations by supporting the training of specialist gender staff to work with or in technical teams.

- Inviting local NGOs to participate in agency meetings and workshops.
- Providing gender-sensitive local NGOs with opportunities to contribute to the design of agency strategies in, and long-term planning for, conflict situations.
- Encouraging agency staff to develop skills as 'trainers of trainers', strengthening local NGOs' ability to explore gender issues in their own work; providing resources such as time, training and technical resources to facilitate this.
- Exploring mechanisms whereby dialogue can be established with local NGOs, so that experience on gender can be incorporated in concrete ways during project design and implementation.
- Encouraging the development of networking between local NGOs on a regional or cross-regional basis.
- Aiming through research and practical experience to discover the concept of gender as it is expressed in each society, and discussing with local NGOs the liberating and oppressive aspects of this concept.
- At grassroots level, seeking out individuals holding moral and spiritual authority who are committed to equity and social justice, and who can become allies, and strengthening them in their work.

(From a paper prepared for a workshop in Thailand, in February 1993, organised by Oxfam on gender issues in situations of conflict.)

Refugee women: their perspectives and our responses

Tina Wallace

Refugee policies are usually developed and implemented without the involvement of refugees. Emergency relief work with refugees — and displaced people — has traditionally been very top-down, involving 'bringing relief to the poor'. The corporate culture and administrative procedures of many aid agencies reflect this approach, which effectively denies access to refugees and prevents dialogue with them even at the grassroots level. In the comparatively few cases where refugees are given some part to play in the delivery of refugee care, they are still excluded from the policy and planning levels; and at the grassroots level women refugees are almost inevitably excluded. Needs and policies are defined, often thousands of miles away, by those who may not have a good understanding of the reality of the situation of the refugees.

It is imperative to change this way of working with refugees, and to take into account their perspectives: not only for policy making and service delivery but also to restore self-respect and self-determination to refugees themselves.

In order to take the women refugees' perspective into account action has to be taken to counteract the factors which have prevented their voice being heard. This means addressing the lack of gender-sensitive staff and policy within aid agencies; undertaking relevant research; learning to involve women in the planning and delivery of refugee assistance; increasing their access to essential goods; working with their own organisations, and learning to listen to them.

Staffing and policy

While there are some women staff concerned about refugee and displaced women to be found in UN and NGO headquarters, they remain few and far between. In 1990 the UNHCR drew up guidelines for working with refugee women which emphasise that programmes 'can be effective only if they are planned with an adequate understanding of, and consultation with, women and their dependents'. (UNHCR, 1990:4)

The guidelines stress the protection and legal rights of women, their need for resources and for special programmes to ensure women's access to them, and the need to employ staff who can integrate this way of working into their area of competence.

Preliminary work on policy in one agency has highlighted the importance of incorporating refugee women from the outset. This means having a competent person on the assessment team to carry out community and gender assessment; recruiting women who can work directly with the refugee women; briefing *all* staff about the issues; setting up women's committees as soon as possible; recruiting women refugees to do health and sanitation work; designing community-based projects in, for example, public health; and evaluating the work from a gender perspective at the end. However, this way of working is still in its earliest stages.

Research

There is only a small body of research and evaluations available within aid agencies which include data on refugee women. There is still very little known about refugee women, especially in new refugee crises. This is not a problem that can be quickly resolved, but it is essential that research institutes and aid agencies start to collect more data on women's issues among refugee populations, and that these data are shared.

There are many sensitivities involved in research with refugees, including the fears of the refugees themselves and of the host government, and concerns about how the data may be used. This is an area where collaborative work with refugee organisations in some cases, and with universities in the host country in others, could fruitfully be developed. Closer links between existing research institutes, both Northern and Southern, and aid agencies could also help in providing information and understanding about all refugee issues, including those of women.

Involving refugee women in decision making

For refugee women to be involved in planning, and making decisions that effect their day-to-day lives is still quite rare. The case studies below illustrate both the cost of this lack of active involvement, and the real potential and benefits of involving women right from the beginning.

The difficulties of involving women

need to be assessed, together with possible ways of overcoming them. These include using female staff, women-only meetings, working with the men to explain the work, and developing and encouraging women's groups. Which strategies are most appropriate will depend on factors, such as cultue, women's workloads and gender relations.

Case study 1: Disregarding women's needs in water distribution

While women are the main collectors and users of water in most camp situations, they are usually excluded from participation in water-supply planning or management. This project was no exception; the work was done by the agency through all-male refugee committees. Water shortages were common in the early days:

'It was clear from discussions with the newly formed Women's Committee ... that they had little idea who was responsible for different aspects of water supply or what the problem had been during the times when there were limited supplies.

During the times of greatest pressure, women were waiting three to four days at the water points to collect water... they could not leave their children to keep their places in the queues, although some women did help each other out by holding places for each other. Most were also busy collecting or buying firewood, taking children to clinics or supplementary feeding centres, cooking, perhaps selling things in the market and carrying out other household activities...

These times of high tension and long queues resulted in frequent fights at water points. Eventually, the Refugee Committee assigned men to assist the water-point watchmen in controlling the women — mainly by standing at the sites and yelling at everyone to stand in order. No attempt was made to discuss the situation with the women or inform them of the problems that were causing the inadequate supply. One

Water–collection point in Hartesheik refugee camp in Sudan. <small>LIBA TAYLOR/OXFAM</small>

cannot help thinking that if the women had been included in these discussions, they might have been more amenable to ... an orderly queuing system... At the very least, the refugee women, who already have a desperate feeling of powerlessness and dependence, were entitled to be informed...' (Hodgkiss, 1989:17-18)

It was recognised during the evaluation of this project that liaising with the refugee community must involve liaising actively with the women too. This community liaison work must be an integral part of one staff person's job description, otherwise the technical problems and demands will always overshadow the social aspects of the work in highly pressurised situations.

Case study 2: Involving women in planning for agriculture

In this case a woman project staff member talked with the women early on in the life of a transit camp. The issues that needed resolving were those of land allocation, and seed and tools distributions. Only two per cent of the camp leaders were women — in spite of the fact that at home women had been organised in women's groups and organisations, and some had leadership skills.

The discussion started by considering the crops the women grew at home and the crops they could grow in the camp which were most like these. The women were actively involved in choosing which seeds they wanted — and these differed from those originally planned — and how they wanted the land allocated. Then they discussed the tools they needed, and it was discovered that the first distribution of hoes had been made only to male household heads, and women-headed households had been excluded.

These discussions led to the setting up of a women's committee which worked with the woman staff member on the seed and land distribution.

During the course of the discussions and distributions, the woman project officer learned a great deal about the survival strategies of these refugee women, knowledge which will be useful in planning viable economic activities for the women in future.

By working in a way that was sensitive to the needs of the women and the men in this situation, women were able to make decisions and take control of issues that critically affected their survival — land, seeds and tool.

Access to essential resources

The resources needed by women differ according to the household structure and the existing gender relations and male/female divisions of consumption and production — for example, who has responsibility for feeding the family. However, in most refugee situations women need proper access to food, materials, land, income-generating activities, training, and health care. Thus, these resources should not be automatically targeted to males. Two case studies below illustrate the possibilities of targeting women directly and the need to include them in education and training schemes in order to enable them to make the best of the resources available.

Cambodian women, displaced from their homes because of fighting between Khmer Rouge and government forces, leaving a distribution point, having been given tools, buckets and other essentials.

MARCUS THOMPSON/OXFAM

Case study 3: Distribution of resources to women

Food, seed and materials distributions can successfully target women in the house-hold (whether as wives or heads-of-households) rather than the men. In this particular case the distribution was carried out through the local structure run by men, and the decisions about allocations were made by men removed from the grassroots situation. While it proved a positive step to give the food directly to the women responsible for provisioning the family, they remained only beneficiaries. They were not actively involved in the distri-bution, had no information about what they were entitled to, and no control over what they received.

The women lacked any decision-making power, and this inevitably led to accusations that food was being misap-propriated before it reached the women. When a subsequent distribution of materials such as hoes and buckets was made, efforts were made to involve a woman staff member, who talked to the women about the allocations and assisted in the distribution. This was much more acceptable to the women.

This illustrates the fact that, for women to have proper access, it was necessary to do more than just target them as benefic-iaries; they also needed to be informed about what was available, and to assist in the distribution.

Case study 4 : The need for training and education

In a project with displaced people, efforts were made to relate to women in the camp through a woman health-officer and the establishment of women's health commit-tees.

However, in spite of the improvement and increase in the water supply, cases of diarrhoeal disease continued to occur. The woman health-worker felt that this needed to be followed up with the women as the problem must relate to issues of water usage.

In many situations, if women are to obtain the full benefit from the resources available, it is not only necessary to talk to women, or to target them, but also to provide education and training about, for example, water, food preparation (where new foods are introduced), agriculture in new conditions, and health care. Usually female rather than male staff will be appropriate for carrying out this work with the women, and often it can best be done by training groups of refugee women.

Building up women's own organisations

In some cases, NGOs can work with and support women's organisations which are already in existence. Examples include: widow's organisations in Guatemala and El Salvador and organisations which specifically work on issues of cultural identity; support for literacy work with women refugees in Sudan through the Eritrean Relief Association and the Relief Society of Tigray; and income generating projects set up through women's organ-isations in the refugee camp, as in Somalia.

Working with refugee organisations, especially those concerned with women, is often a slow process demanding time and support from agency staff. The need for a change of pace as refugee situations develop is critical. All too often it is the initial emergency requirement for speed that continues to dominate the way in which agencies work. This militates against involving refugees, especially women, and can set up patterns that prove impossible to break later. Learning to work with refugee organisations demands a change of approach.

In many situations women's groups do not exist and so need to be developed. The following case is one where this was done undervery difficult circumstance, where women feared to be known as refugees for security reasons.

Case study 5: Forming a group to deal with mental health problems

A project was started some years ago to work with Guatemalan refugee women in Mexico city. They were suffering from a range of physical and mental health problems common to refugees. A small group of women was established which began by looking at their lives and trying to answer questions such as: Why are we poor? Why are we malnourished? From looking at their poor health they moved into wider issues which enabled the women to put their very negative feelings and experiences into a wider context. They came to see that their reactions were normal in an abnormal situation. The women learnt a great deal over a long period — it was a slow and painful process — and then decided to produce a booklet on ways to live in Mexico, and their perspective on the need for change at home and in their gender roles.

This project had to work to develop the group and to work gradually through the women's trauma in order to focus on improving their mental health. Women could only start this process once they had the confidence to work together as a group.

Listening to women

The process of listening to women has started at international and national level with the calling of conferences involving refugees, for example, in Costa Rica, Mexico and at the World Council of Churches in Geneva. It also takes place at grassroots level in some projects..

Listening to women can lead agencies in directions they did not expect; in Mozambique women prioritised clothes as their major need, while in Uganda a research project on conflict and suffering in war led to rape counselling being identi-

fied as the urgent need for women. In both cases this was not what agency staff or the researchers had originally planned to deliver.

When women are consulted, issues of education, cultural identity and psychological health are frequently stressed, yet these issues are largely overlooked in much refugee work. Listening to women requires time and the design of appropriate structures for meetings — or using existing channels previously overlooked — employing staff who are ready to talk and listen, and being willing to change policy and practice where necessary.

Work for the future

There is a need for many changes in the way refugee work is perceived and carried out. As women refugees have argued, these changes will lead to better, more appropriate programmes in future.

There is a need for wide-ranging research into the situation of refugee women in different areas. Indicators for needs' assessment must be devised. Agencies need guidance as to what indicators they can use in an emergency in order quickly to assess women refugees' basic needs.

There is also a need for research into women's changing roles and responsibilities as refugees Gender relations often change dramatically in times of crisis.

Training of staff working with refugees is necessary, to enable them to listen to women, and to design programmes taking them into account. Training programmes should cover decision-makers, policy-makers and planners, as well as field workers.

Staff should be recruited who understand the issues and can work directly with refugee women. In most countries these staff should be women, drawn from the host or refugee society.

Time needs to be allowed for working

with refugee women, and developing structures for this where they do not exist. Effort should be made to listen and learn from all refugees — including the women. Refugees should be seen not as passive recipients of aid, but as active participants, people who develop their own survival strategies and who do most of the work for themselves. The agencies need to act in a way which affirms, rather than denies that.

Adapted from a paper written in September 1990 by Tina Wallace, then in Oxfam's Gender and Development Unit, for a seminar at the Institute for Development Studies in The Hague, Netherlands. Tina Wallace is currently the Coordinator of Oxfam's Planning and Evaluation Unit.

Refugee women in Saba'ad Camp, Somalia, selling 'basta' (spaghetti), flour, rice, and onions. Refugees are not simply passive recipients of aid, but actively pursue their own survival strategies.
JEREMY HARTLEY/OXFAM

References

Ball, C (1991) 'When broken heartedness becomes a political issue' in *Changing Perceptions: Writings on Gender and Development*, Oxford, Oxfam.

Berry, B (1988) 'Refugee Women Case Study: Somalia' paper prepared for the International Consultation on Refugee Women in Geneva, November.

Camus J G (1986) 'Refugee women: the forgotten majority', Oxford, Queen Elizabeth House, November.

Demeke, T (1990) 'Refugee women's survival strategies and prostitution in Eastern Sudan', in *Refugee Participation Network* 7.

Ferris, E (1988) 'A background paper on refugee women' prepared for the International Consultation on Refugee Women in Geneva, November.

Ferris, E (1990) 'Refugee women and violence', Geneva, World Council of Churches.

Hall, E (1988) *Vocational training for women refugees in Africa: guidelines from selected field projects*, Training Policies Discussion Paper 26, Geneva, International Labour Organisation.

Hodgkiss, P (1989) 'Somali refugee programme (Ethiopia) evaluation report' for Oxfam, unpublished.

Kelly, N (1989) *Working with Refugee Women: A Practical Guide*, Geneva, International NGO Working Group on Refugee Women.

McGregor, J A and Adam, A (1990) 'Refugee women: the Port Sudan small scale Enterprise Programme', *Refugee Participation Network* 7.

Neugue, L M D (1988) *Run for your life: peasant tales of tragedy in Mozambique*, Trenton, Africa World Press.

Report on the National Conference of Refugee Women, Mexico, November 1989.

Truong, T-D (1990) *Refugee perspective: Issues and Concerns*, The Hague, Institute for Social Studies.

UNHCR Guidelines on working with refugee women, May 1990.

Urdang, S (1989) *And still they dance: women, war and the struggle for change in Mozambique*, London, Earthscan Publications.

Women's Commission for Refugee Women and Children (1990) 'Report of the Delegation of the Commission to Hong Kong', January 5-12.

Working with women refugees in eastern Sri Lanka

Nalini Kasynathan

Sri Lanka has experienced continuous conflict for more than a decade. The war in the north-east has claimed tens of thousands of lives, caused extensive damage to infrastructure and led to massive displacement of people. Over 1.5 million people are displaced internally, of whom 250,000 are living in camps within Sri Lanka; 50,000 people have fled to Canada, 210,000 to India officially and probably another 150,000 unofficially, 100,000 to Europe and 10,000 to Australia. People continue to be displaced as villages are attacked either by the government security forces, para-military groups, Home Guards or the militant groups.

Community Aid Abroad (CAA) started working in the Batticaloa district in eastern Sri Lanka in January 1991 with displaced people who had lost their homes, livelihood and some of their family members. Following major fighting between the government forces and the militant groups in this district, which began in June 1990, 30,000 persons fled into the jungle, 150,000 others moved out of their villages and went to live with friends and relatives in and around the town, and 50,000 more took refuge in government-run camps.

With funding provided by the Australian Government, CAA started a relief and rehabilitation programme for 2,000 families, providing them with basic shelter materials, cooking utensils, agri-cultural implements, seeds and fertilisers. The programme initially was not gender-specific; it aimed at helping those displaced to resettle in their new environment. People were organised into groups and given the essentials to start life again. Distribution of protein supplements for mothers and children was an important component of the programme.

While the displaced men could not find any employment and tended to remain idle, the women took up the main burden of caring for the family. They picked grain from fields harvested the previous year; nursed children who were suffering from malaria, diarrhoea, and many other infectious diseases; fetched drinking water and gathered firewood.

Loans requested for agriculture

At the end of six months, an evaluation was done to assess the efficiency of the programme. The women, especially, indicated that they would prefer a portion of the funds previously allocated for consumable items to be given instead in the form of loans for agriculture. CAA agreed to provide agricultural assistance to the families, particularly to the women. As it was mainly women who were involved, vegetable cultivation, rather than rice-growing, was identified as the most suitable income-generating activity. It was possible for women to participate fully, as vegetables could be grown around their houses, and watering and tillage was therefore manageable.

During the first season many families were able to earn between 1500 and 2000 rupees from vegetable cultivation in addition to meeting their own consumption needs. Following this success, the programme was expanded to include another 700 families. Agricultural extension officers provided advice and training. Functional literacy skills, health education, and basic financial management were also included in the programme.

After a year, it was clear that the women and their families had grown out of the relief phase of their resettlement. By this time, 47 societies had been formed with a total of 1800 members, 70 per cent of whom

were women. These societies elected a central executive committee of five members to manage the programme; four of them were women. At the request of the committee, CAA assisted in establishing handloom centres and providing skills-training in cane handicraft, and the preservation and processing of agricultural produce.

Soon the women members began to see inadequacies in the way the credit programme was run. CAA's partner organisation in the programme was not easily or readily accessible. Furthermore, the women felt that they were being excluded from the decision-making processes in the organisation. They called a general meeting of the membership, discussed their concerns openly and decided to form their own organisation to implement the second phase of the project.

Muslim woman, beside her burnt–out home, after an outbreak of violence in Eastern Province, Sri Lanka.
JEFF ALDERSON/OXFAM

Lessons learned

CAA's work confirms that in times of war and total disruption, as has happened in eastern Sri Lanka, it is both necessary and efficient to work with women. In war situations women and children are the most affected and most in need. More than 40 per cent of the women in the project area had become heads of their households, because their husbands had been disabled, or killed, were fighting with one or the other of the warring factions, had disappeared or were hiding to avoid arrest or conscription. The men remaining in the village, unable to carry out their traditional occupations, did not have sufficient resourcefulness to cope. The immediacy of women's feelings for the survival of their families gave them the initiative and flexibility to find new resources.

Participating in income-generating activities, and taking responsibility for others in an environment of collective action, served as effective therapy for women who had been traumatised by the conflict. Engaging in collective and meaningful work enabled them to recover sanity and dignity. In a war situation, when everything else has been lost, it is even more important to encourage reliance on the only thing that is left, that is, the will to survive.

War provides an opportunity for women's empowerment. The disruption of established structures, guidelines and taboos has made room for women to move into areas from which they were previously excluded. The challenge is to make women conscious of the empowerment issues so that the gains they have made survive the war. Therefore, empowerment must be seen as a continuing process, through women organising themselves collectively with an understanding of their position. Workwith women must not confine itself to relief work and to trauma counselling. It must deliberately seek to build on the urgency and the opportunities provided by the situation of war. Income-generation activities must be used to build women's organisations, which focus on conscious empowerment.

It is important to distinguish between the practical difficulties of working in hazardous areas and the suitability or otherwise of income-generation and organisational work in war situations. It is not true that only disaster relief work can be done in such situations. In fact, CAA's work in Sri Lanka has shown that development work may be the most effective way of dealing with the damage caused by protracted war.

Author's note:

In writing this paper, I have drawn extensively on factual information in field reports, and on a paper by Shanthi Sachidananthan, CAA's Project Officer in Sri Lanka.

Nalini Kasynathan is Programme Director for South-East Asia for Community Aid Abroad.

The psychosocial effects of 'La Violencia' on widows of El Quiché, Guatemala

Judith Zur

This is a brief account of the psychosocial impact of the civil war in Guatemala on Quiché Maya Indian Women and is based on 20 months' anthropological research with widows from the department of El Quiché between the years 1988-1990.

Guatemalan Mayan Indian women have been affected by government-sponsored terrorism directed at Guatemala's civilian population during the years 1980-1983 (called *La Violencia*), as a counterinsurgency strategy in the 30-year civil war. The strategy consisted of army 'scorched-earth' tactics including incursions into the villages, indiscriminate torture and killing of individuals, families and even entire communities. A subsequent, so-called, 'low intensity warfare' continues to the present day, involving random government-sponsored terrorism by medium to small military units that sneak up on isolated rural settlements.

Between 1978 and 1985 at least 112,000 political killings and 18,000 'disappearances' were carried out by army, police, and paramilitary government forces (GVIS, 1992).[1] Over the past two decades at least 120,000 women have been widowed in Guatemala, many of whom have also lost other relatives.

The province of El Quiché was among the most severely affected areas of the country and approximately 11,000 widows were left in this department alone. Its people bore the brunt of selective guerrilla actions followed by further army retaliations in the form of public village-massacres and other atrocities. These were carried out by army irregulars — the local 'voluntary' civil patrols, a coerced and unpaid service. The patrols, organised under local chiefs, installed in all villages in 1982, served as the army's eyes and ears, though ostensibly they were set up to eradicate 'subversives' and 'bandits' in the local area. After carrying out a massacre they silenced villagers by threatening them that if they spoke about what had happened they would suffer further violence. Their activities effectively destroyed all social relationships, networks, and solidarity among civilian populations.

It is difficult to generalise about the meaning of war and its psychosocial effects, because they are determined by the particular manifestations of violence within each village, which depend on the vagaries of the social structure, culture and history of the village, and the characteristics of the local perpetrators of violence. For example, violence tended to operate along the divisions between factions already existing within any particular village. The meaning of war and its psychosocial effects are also determined by the attitude of the state with reference to any specific group of people, in this case, women. The position of women in the family, the kinship structure, and the

Civil patrol, Cobán.

ANA CECILIA GONZALEZ/OXFAM

fact that they were widows (now deemed 'wives of the guerrillas') related to the type of violence encountered, not only during the drastic experienceof *La Violencia* but also in the course of subsequent events.

La Violencia became a crisis in the everyday life of the community. An explicit and implicit renegotiation of power took place, with the chiefs controlling the village along with the military commissioners (local men who remain in the pay of the army after completing military service), who displaced civil authorities, catechists, health promoters and teachers.

The impact of *La Violencia* went far beyond the years of violence. For *La Violencia* did not erupt and then disappear, it was a continual source of insecurity in women's lives. This was not only because of the sporadic incidents of violence, which continue to the present. There was also intimidation of women from within the community, in the form of threats to their

lives, and sexual harassment by the local men who had killed their relatives. Women were threatened with further rape, and with death; and they knew that the threats were not idle. Any woman who joined a human rights organisation such as GAM,[2] CONAVIGUA[3] or CERJ[4] or even 'neutral' NGOs (non-governmental organisations), were threatened with kidnapping or death, for themselves or their children. The range of violence they suffered ranged from abuse and obscenities thrown at them to further murders or kidnapping of their relatives or themselves. There was also symbolic violence, in the shape of the imposition of forms of language, such as euphemisms and Spanish terms which were never explained, by the dominant forces, and the internalisation of state repression. On several levels, then, the violence has had repercussions which far exceed the moment of its occurrence.

The divisions which existed in the

community along religious grounds proliferated and intensified. There are now rifts and mutual suspicion among groups of women, for example, between those who participate in human rights organisations and those who do not. Internalisation of this divisive tendency, which the army built upon in order to prevent the formation of resistance groups, led to splits between the groups of women themselves. They fought over many things including men and aid. The scarcity of men in the village meant that, even if they wanted to, women had little opportunity to remarry. Some chose not to marry, in order to honour the dead and to avoid the violent 'macho' stance which has been strengthened by men's internalisation of military attitudes.

These problems were mainly between widows and non-widows, for among themselves the widows displayed considerable dignity in the way that they requested and received aid. Resentments built up between women when a widow managed to survive without a man and a married woman felt threatened in case the widow should steal her husband. On the other hand, those who had lost their husbands and sons suspected that others in the community had betrayed them. The conflicts were further intensified from in-fighting among families who felt entitled to the land of those who had died, and to aid offered by agencies.

What the violence and loss meant for widows was a virtual reformulation of family life. This took place at various levels, from the roles taken up by women and children to replace those of missing male kin, to attitudinal changes regarding the security that one could expect from the family. The threat to the family meant that members had to disperse spatially in order to survive (owing to an efficient intelligence network, they were often traced and then 'disappeared'). As a result of witnessing relatives being massacred, and being unable to respond, women's images of themselves

as mothers and wives, and as carers and complementary partners, respectively, were destroyed. On a practical level, women had to become the household head, the main bread-winner and generally take over men's responsibilities, particularly if all the grown men in the family were dead or missing. This not only meant an extra workload for women who already worked tremendously hard but also the humiliation of taking on men's tasks in a society with a strict division of labour. The reformulation of family life also meant, in turn, that the relationship to the past was altered.

The over-riding emotion I encountered in the women was fear. When a war is waged by a hostile, foreign force, the members of a community can use their national or ethnic identity to rally their members in self-defence. When civil war is waged, however, the identification of the enemy, as well as the organisation of self-defence, is more problematic. And terror is made even more intense when a population faces government-sponsored terrorism perpetrated by an extension of the army in the form of local villagers themselves; and when human rights and the due process of law are suspended by the very institution claiming to be their guardians.

The deaths and disappearances which have taken place over the years, and especially the massacres they witnessed, created a new awareness among the survivors of their vulnerability. This was heightened by the fact that killers and victims continued to live in close proximity. It was not an anonymous person or crowd who had done the killing. The killers were known and continued to be the authorities in the village. The bodies of the dead were also hidden in clandestine graves which people were forbidden to approach. One of the many questions that haunted the living was how to fulfil their obligations towards the dead, because they had been deprived of the opportunity to bury them properly. In the case of the 'disappeared', not knowing the where-abouts of a relative causes immense distress, fear and near paralysis.

The war experience has also politicised women. It has made them aware that with their passive stance towards the political problems and their 'lack of ideas', they were as harmful as those who acted wrongly and brought the enemy to the village. Many also realised that violence and war created more problems for woman than for men, and that men did not care about women's problems, nor about abandoning women.

The women who were best off were those who began to comprehend the violence in political terms through participation in human rights agencies and women's groups, notwithstanding the risks involved; those who began to learn to read and write and to speak Spanish and gained confidence in negotiating with the outside male/*ladino* world; and those from the handful of villages where exhumations took place, because they could bury their dead in a dignified and proper way.

Psychological symptoms among women resulting from the experience of so much pain were mostly expressed in a physical way. Women's problems took the form of headaches, stomach aches, back aches and general pains throughout the body. It is difficult to separate these out from the pain which comes as a result of arduous work and malnutrition, given the impoverished conditions in which Indian families live. However, I believe that the pain women suffer in their bodies reflects the fact that they have become the repositories of painful experiences — experiences which they have been unable to articulate both because they have been silenced and also because of the impossibility of speaking about such atrocious experiences.

Notes

1   Guatemala Geo-violence Information Systems, c/o Guatemala Human Rights Commission, Washington DC.
2   Grupo Apoyo Mutuo.
3   Coordinacion Nacional de los Viudas Guatemaltecas.
4   Comite de los Etnias, Runujel Junam.

Judith Zur is a psychologist and anthropologist. She worked in El Quiche from 1988–90 and is writing a book on Guatemalan war widows. She also works as a family therapist at the Medical Foundation for the Care of Victims of Torture, in London

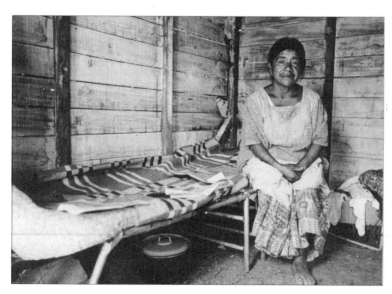

A widow in her home in El Mezquital, Guatemala City.

ANA CECILIA GONSALEZ /OXFAM

'Clutching a knifeblade'
Human rights and development from Asian women's perspective

Nelia Sancho-Liao

There is a popular Filipino idiomatic expression that aptly describes the plight of the majority of Filipino women and those of other Asian countries. The expression is *kapit sa patalim*. Literally, it means 'clutching a knifeblade'. For the Filipino, these words sum up a person's utter despair, and the sacrifice called for under extreme adversities. It describes what women or men, in their helplessness, would do in response to their human desire to continue living today and, perhaps, for another day.

Kapit sa patalim is the situation of thousands of Filipino domestic helpers who were stranded in the deserts of Iraq and Kuwait two years ago. Some of them were raped at the height of chaos and war because they hesitated to leave the country immediately for fear of losing their once-in-a-lifetime, dollar-paying jobs.

Kapit sa patalim is the lot of 16,000 Filipino girls, mostly coming from landless peasant families in the provinces, who have become prostitutes, catering to the sexual whims of American servicemen in Clark Air base and Subic Naval Base, both US military installations in the Philippines. These girls thought that perhaps, through luck and hard work, they might some day land a more dignified and better-paying job, but most of them have ended up afflicted with sexually transmitted diseases, including AIDS, and more destitute than when they first came to the city looking for work.

Kapit sa patalim describes the circumstances of women workers in foreign-owned garment factories in the Bataan export-processing zone in the Philippines, who are forced to work in 36-hour shifts during which they are allowed only two hours' sleep and a few minutes' break each day.

This Filipino expression also applies to the similar state of despair and sacrifice required of women in other Asian countries. It aptly describes the experience of tens of thousands of Sri Lankan women who migrate to countries in the Middle East to work as nannies and domestic helpers; of 200,000 Nepali women who earn a living in various brothels of India; of Indonesian women workers employed in transnational factories, half of whom are afflicted with kidney ailments because of mercury contamination in and around their factories.

Kapit sa patalim describes the victims of wife abuse in Papua New Guinea, who represent, according to a reform law committee, 67 per cent of the country's rural women and 56 per cent of its urban women; it describes the battered wives in Bangladesh who, despite their husbands' cruelty, would not file for divorce nor leave home because in their country separated, abandoned, or divorced women are considered social outcasts; it describes the Indian brides threatened by dowry death, which, according to estimates made by the Ahmedabad Women's Action Group, reached 1,000 in 1988 in one state alone; it describes the Indian mothers of 78,000 female foetuses who, succumbing to a dominant cultural bias against female children, agreed to an abortion after undergoing sex-determination tests.

Extreme, but not uncommon, situations such as these underscore the pathetic state of women's human rights in Asia. If these cases are so gross and skewed, if these are too concentrated forms of discrimination and violence against our gender, it is because Asian women live on the margins of a region where two-thirds of humanity exist in hunger and squalor. They have actually been pushed to the edge where every human being's rights to dignity, to life and development are not only pieces of empty rhetoric but have become cruel ironies. In Asia, women are on the margins of the margins.

Women have borne the brunt of the adverse consequences of complex historical processes of economic stagnation and exploitation plaguing most Asian nations. These processes have denied the peoples of the region their most basic rights. The denial, however, is of a bigger dimension for women.

From the impoverished countryside to the city slums

Most Asian countries are agricultural economies, with the majority of the population living in rural areas, where landlessness has increased at an alarming rate, pushing down the wages of farm workers and intensifying competition for the limited number of jobs available. These trends have been most burdensome for rural women because, following tradition, they receive less pay for agricultural work and have fewer job opportunities than men.

Massive urban immigration of unskilled rural labourers owing to increasing landlessness and low productivity of agriculture has been particularly harsh on women. In many cities most jobs are low-paying and there is a huge army of unemployed people. While both men and women migrants have difficulty in finding jobs in the cities, men usually land more stable and better-paid jobs, such as those in construction and in small factories. Women have to take low-paid jobs as domestic helpers or street vendors, if they manage to find gainful employment at all.

The high urban migration rate in Asian countries has resulted in rapid and unplanned urbanisation, exhausting the basic services delivery systems in the cities and causing severe overcrowding. The number of slums and squatter areas has risen dramatically in recent years in major Asian cities.

Women in export-processing zones

The thrusts of Asian governments' development policies have also been discriminatory to women. In the last two decades, several governments in the region have set up export-processing zones: industrial enclaves designed to attract transnational corporations by providing them with necessary infrastructures and 'most-favoured status', guaranteeing them various exemptions from tax, labour, and wage regulations.

Most workers in the foreign-owned factories in these export-processing zones are women. Their traditional docility and their vulnerability to physical, psychological, and sexual harassment are characteristics exploited by employers to prevent the growth of trade unionism in these enclaves. Asian women generally receive only a fraction of the salary paid to

Shanty town, Manila.

workers in industrialised Western countries; their basic wage level, with the exception of Japan and Singapore, represents only about half of the amount needed for a decent family life, and this has even diminished in the last ten years; and moreover, women workers earn less than their male counterparts.

Tourism: a cloak for prostitution

The aggressive and misoriented promotion of tourism is another government 'development' thrust that has been extremely inimical to women. The aim is to make the tourist industry a principal dollar-earner for Asian economies. Promotional schemes such as those of Thailand and the Philippines often stress 'service attractions', which tacitly include sex services.

Prostitution in Asian countries, of course, did not start with tourism; the problem is made worse by extreme under-development and vestiges of colonialism. But prostitution has certainly been aggravated by government tourism schemes. There are reported to be as many as 800,000 child prostitutes in Thailand, and 400,000 adult and child prostitutes in the Philippines.

The presence of US military bases in the region have led to an increase in prostitution. In the Philippines, for example, a decent job inside these foreign military installations is not possible for Filipino women. They earn a living as prostitutes in 'amusement places' around the immediate vicinity of the two largest American bases.

Bangladesh. Women showing their bruises, after being beaten up by the police. They were trying to claim their legal right to land. One said 'You see us with our heads covered today, but on the day of the demonstration our heads were bare and we were ready to fight for what is our right.'   SUE GREIG/OXFAM

Political repression

Political repression, a characteristic feature of both the authoritarian regimes and the elite democracies common to Asian countries, is particularly wicked to women. In an effort to stem serious social strife arising from mass poverty and popular dissatisfaction, many governments of the region have adopted stringent legislation curtailing mass protests, trade unions and political associations, and freedom of expression. While these measures whittle down the democratic rights of both women and men alike, the way in which they are enforced on women by men in authority is strongly influenced by male aggression and machismo.

Thus women trade unionists, peasant activists, poor urban protestors, community workers, and militant students not only suffer arrest, detention, and physical torture. In addition, they have to

endure sexual harassment, molestation, and even rape from their captors. In the Philippines, there are reports that wives of political prisoners are asked for sexual favours by military guards in exchange for being allowed to see their husbands. An intensifying policy of state repression in many Asian countries provides male enforcers with a powerful political rationale and plenty of opportunities for unleashing sexual aggression against women.

Civil wars in a number of Asian countries have caused serious distress to women. In the Philippines, for instance, the Aquino government has launched a policy of total war against all suspected guerrilla strongholds in the countryside. Today there are more than 200,000 internal refugees in the country. They are mostly women and children. Their husbands, brothers, and grown-up sons have been forced to migrate temporarily to faraway provinces to escape constant harassment by the military.

Patriarchy and male domination, prevalent in traditional Asian societies, have also spawned widespread gender-specific crimes such as rape, physical assault, wife-beating, and dowry deaths. These crimes recognise no distinction of race, class, or ethnic origin, only the fact that the target of violence is a woman. In most Asian countries religion, culture, laws and courts, as well as public opinion, discriminate against victims of gender crimes. These traditional institutions favour the male assailants – a reality that inhibits victims from fighting back and forces most women to suffer in silence.

Military sexual slavery

One major current issue we are now working on in Asia is the issue of military sexual slavery, perpetrated by the Japanese Imperial Army during World War II. This issue has resulted in an Asia-wide campaign on the part of the Asian Women's Human Rights Council together with organisations in Korea, Taipei or Taiwan, and in the Philippines.

There are an estimated 200,000 Asian women who were conscripted as 'comfort women' by Japan from 1942 to 1945. Eighty per cent of the women were from North and South Korea, which were provinces of Japan at the time.

The Asian women were raped, tortured, and massacred by Japanese troops. The use of 'comfort women' is a form of sexual slavery, a war crime against Asian women, and illustrates how women are system-atically abused and degraded sexually, physically, and psychologically by milit-arism and war.

For 50 years the Japanese government kept its involvement in the conscription and procurement of the Asian 'comfort women' hidden. But they kept documents and records, and in the last two years private researchers have uncovered these sources and presented them as evidence against the Japanese government. It was only in July 1992 that the Japanese Foreign Minister finally admitted Japan's responsibility and publicly apologised for this war crime. The case was also presented at the UN Sub-Commission on Human Rights in August 1992, and a Committee on Post-War Compensation has been set up to study what could be done to redress the violation of women's human rights.

These crimes recognise no distinction of race, class, or ethnic origin, only the fact that the target of violence is a woman.

Only now have women started speaking out, with the support of the women's movement in Asia, after the 50 years of shame and silence that they have had to suffer because of Asian patriarchal culture. But military sexual slavery and violence against women is still going on today in the current war in the former Yugoslavia, for instance. It happened to 200,000 Bangladeshi women in the Bangladeshi/Pakistani border war. It is also the experience of some 12,000 Bhutanese refugees in Nepal, who have been raped by Bhutanese soldiers; and of women in the Philippines in the context of the Philippines government's 'total war policy'.

We are demanding that the United Nations and the international community address this issue. The women's movement around the world needs to study the phenomenon more closely and to adopt recommendations to governments and the United Nations system to create effective safeguards to prevent the occurrence of this war crime.

The Asian Women's Human Rights Council

Because of the massive problems we are facing not only on this issue but on other human rights violations against women, the Asian Women's Human Rights Council was set up as an addition to three regional commissions of women's organisations in Asia. We feel that we cannot be content with just presenting the image of women as victims. We feel that Asian women have a big role to play in changing their situation, and the AWHRC is a result of this belief. We have come together in order to bring a human rights perspective to development concerns. In the next three years, AWHRC is planning a series of six tribunals: public hearings to highlight important issues to women in Asia. The tribunals will tackle the following issues:

- Sex trafficking (Japan, May 1993)
- Violence against women (Pakistan, December 1993)
- Militarism, environment, and violence against women (Korea, March 1994)
- Crimes of development against women in Asia (India)
- Religion and violence against women (Malaysia, 1994)
- Indigenous women (December 1994).

Conclusion

This, in brief, is the human rights situation of the majority of women in Asia. I believe that the advocacy of women's human rights in the region should be put in this perspective. Advocacy of the human rights of Asian women should deal effectively with the fact that the strong system of patriarchy and male domination in the region has made the burden of oppression and exploitation of women far worse and more unbearable than that of men. Women constantly face violence and assaults on their dignity and their lives *simply because they are women.*

Advocacy of human rights for Asian women should mean, in addition, working for their total liberation from all the forces that oppress them and ensuring their development and empowerment. It should mean opposing the domination and exploitation of poor nations by a few rich and powerful ones, and promoting a new world economic order and the genuine development of Third World countries.

It should include working for the eradication of the unjust and repressive structures of most Asian societies and promoting an equitable distribution of wealth and the development of democracy and popular initiative. It should involve a consistent struggle against patriarchy and male domination in all their manifestations, to raise the status of women as coequal partners of men in all spheres of life.

And, most important of all, human rights work to deal effectively with women's human rights violations involves of necessity empowering women themselves. There is a need to support the proliferation of women's initiatives and resistance, harness women's creative energies to analyse and to work on strategies, whether this be at the personal level, the community and national level, or the regional and international level.

Nelia Sancho-Liao has been involved in the popular movement in the Philippines for 20 years, more than half of that working in the areas of women's and children's rights. She was a political prisoner for over two years and through that experience she has become involved in the defence of human rights for political prisoners. She has worked for democratisation and people's empowerment and is now the Regional Coordinator of the Asian Women's Human Rights Council, an Asia-wide organisation promoting a new understanding of human rights and development, based on the realities of Asian women.

Domestic violence as a development issue

Ruth Jacobson

In development theory, there are some interesting analogies between the 'discovery' in the 1960s and 1970s of women as economically productive[1] and current concern around domestic violence against women. This has major policy implications for development organisations in the North and raises complex and difficult questions. Northern women's movements have engaged with the issue within an analytical framework which changed the prevalent terms of discourse but which was also subject to eurocentric bias and racist stereotyping.[2]

Western agencies need to take steps to define what constitutes their specific legitimate areas of concern. An initial step would be to ensure that work already being done by Southern women (and some men) is given practical support and made accessible to their constituencies. This process is under way in some organisations (see for example GADU's *Newspack* 15) but needs consistent monitoring to ensure that it does not become marginalised as 'another women's issue'. This could be an appropriate task for all supporters of Oxfam and the other British Third World NGOs at local level.

Once the material is made accessible, then the question is how to use it effectively. One approach could be to look at areas of commonality and difference. Work being done by Third World women contains a number of features which also resonate in the North. Among these are:

- Domestic violence in the Third World, as in Britain, cannot meaningfully be described as 'abnormal' in its incidence or social acceptability but available statistics are very often misleading.[3]
- Contrary to many stereotypes, it is not confined to any one particular socio-economic class but is closely associated with male control of female sexuality and culturally-specific definitions of 'women's place'. Women all over the world are subject to an implicit contract whereby their societies offer them economic and social security provided they do not breach these boundaries — find your own examples![4]
- Theories based on a single premise such as 'All men are violent' or 'modern-isation is to blame' are inadequate, and women must be prepared to confront the complicity of other women in some forms of violence.[5]
- These commonalities must not lull us into universalising notions of 'women's oppression', ignoring factors of race, ethnicity and class. To take just one example, Western analyses frequently refer to battered 'wives', with an assumption that domestic violence takes place only within a (heterosexual) partnership. In other contexts, however, women may be assaulted by brothers, uncles or male in-laws.

In looking at areas of concern, development agencies must further be prepared to confront the fact that their interventions may affect those power relations which are inseparable from domestic violence. Investigating these would involve raising questions of project planning, monitoring and evaluation. In the past, these have generally been regarded as a professional preserve, but under the new language of accountability should become part of an open agenda.

A case study contained in my original paper[6] looked at the result of intervention by a NGO in a Sri Lankan village. For most households, women's economic contribution was vital for survival and this principally took the form of processing cashew nuts for domestic and export sales. The sexual division of labour was marked so, despite high unemployment, men would not consider doing cashew-nut processing themselves.

The NGO in question was small-scale, sensitive to local culture (with joint involvement of Christian and Buddhist clergy), and reliable access to outside funds — the ideal project partner. It even took women's economic needs as a priority from the outset. A loan scheme was established, on much more helpful terms than the village money lenders, to allow women to expand processing in their homes. The scheme certainly achieved its initial objectives: not only did women who borrowed from the fund significantly expand their production and income; this had the effect of pushing up the wages of those women who continued to process cashew nuts for wages. As a result 'the remarkable increases in income were clearly manifested in improved living conditions, particularly in housing.'

So far, this would seem to read like a text-book example of a 'good' development scheme. Yet the authors took the unusual step of being prepared to evaluate it from the perspective of gender relations, and here they identified a problematic area. Noting that the increase in women's incomes was taking place in the context of male unemployment, they concluded that 'the impetus given by the credit facilities of the Gampubuduwa Village Society *has accelerated the disparities in the expected and actual roles of men and women.*' (my emphasis) This was illustrated by the fact that village women are convinced that alcohol consumption by village men was higher than in other areas without the credit scheme. One case study concerned a woman who became so successful through the credit scheme that she felt able to consider a legal separation from her violent husband. The hostility this aroused from her husband and his friends is such that she is now branded as 'hard' and allegations of prostitution are made against her. (At the same time, it should be noted that another instance is given of a couple where the husband is actively supporting his wife's new economic role.)

The object of this analysis is not, of course, to argue against credit schemes for women but to reinforce the point already made in other GADU publications, such as *Changing Perceptions*, that interventions by development agencies are rarely, if ever, gender-neutral. Project staff who are seriously concerned with gender equality must be prepared to tackle this issue, as must those staff who produce publicity and information material for home consumption.

What then constitutes a 'legitimate' concern? Given the overwhelming prevalence of negative and racist images of Third World societies in the British media, development agencies have understandable reservations about how explicit their material should be on the topic of domestic violence. On the other hand, surely sensitively presented information on, for example, the work being done by groups like SOS Corpo in Brazil could be a constructive contribution to the empowerment of women. For me, the only 'non-legitimate' response would be to keep the issue hidden.

Notes

1 This paper is adapted from a longer one whose starting point was an analogy between the ways in which women's economic participation was largely 'invisible' until the work of Boserup, Beneria, Dixon-Mueller.

2 Amina Mama, author of the first comprehensive study of domestic violence against black women in Britain, comments on 'the lack of material which considered black women's specific experience in any depth. Where references to black women were found, they were often incidental, relegated to a footnote and more often than not perpetuated stereotypical notions such as the passive Asian women and the strong matriarchal African/Caribbean women.' (Mama 1989 p xi)

3 The difficulties in reaching some sort of quantifiable base line are very complex. Jahan covers some of them in her comment on reports in the Bangladeshi press from 1980-1984 which appear to show an increase from 12.4 to 32.7 per cent in the proportion of women in the total number of victims of violence: 'It is unclear, however, whether the noted increase in crime reflects an actual increase in the number and frequency of incidents during this period or whether it reflects better coverage resulting from pressures from women's groups.' (Janan 1989 p198)

4 There can be instances where the simple fact of women being together constitutes a threat to male control. Thus, in Ethiopia, women's everyday coffee gatherings provide an opportunity to 'think about, and to some extent define, their own lives and positions in society' and as a result 'many husbands beat their wives to stop them participating' — to no effect! (Selassie 1984 p14)

5 The work of Third World feminists on dowry is of particular relevance: 'In many instances, the in-laws and co-wives, instead of intervening, actively aid and abet the husband in his violence against the wife. ... the in-laws may take on the responsibility of chastisement, which may end in severe injury or even death.' (Jahan p215)

6 The following section is a highly compressed version of material presented in the paper by Casinder, Fernando & Gamage in Momsen and Townsend *Geography of Gender in the Third World*.

References

Agarwal, B (ed) (1988) *Structures of Patriarchy*, London, Zed Books.

Casinder, Fernando and Gamage (1987) ' Women's Issues and men's roles: Sri Lankan village experience' in Momsen and Townsend (eds) (1987) *Geography of Gender in the Third World*.

Jahan, R (1988) 'Hidden wounds, visible scars: violence against women in Bangladesh' in Agarwal (ed) (1988) op.cit.

Mama, Amina (1989) *The Hidden Struggle: statutory and voluntary sector responses to violence against black women in the home* London, London Race and Housing Research Unit.

Momsen J and Townsend J (eds) (1987) *Geography of Gender in the Third World*, London, Hutchinson.

Selassie, T (1984) *In search of Ethiopian Women*, Change International Report No 11, London.

Ruth Jacobson is a researcher on gender issues in Southern Africa, currently working on gender and democratisation. She has worked in Mozambique as a teacher and community development worker. She is currently at the Department of Peace Studies at the University of Bradford.

Forced prostitution of women and girls in Brazil

Anti-Slavery International

This is adapted from a submission by Anti-Slavery International to the United Nations Economic and Social Council Commission on Human Rights, Sub-Commission on Prevention of Discrimination and Protection of Minorities Working Group on Contemporary Forms of Slavery, Seventeenth Session, Geneva 1992.

In the last five years there have been increasing reports of 'white slavery' and of a traffic in women and young girls enticed from towns in the south of Pará and Maranhão States to work in brothels near mining encampments and large civil construction projects. The question of child prostitution is not limited to the north of the country, but information about such activity in the region has recently been given greater public attention. In 1987 the State Deputy João Batista repeatedly tried to draw the attention of state and federal authorities to conditions of lawlessness in Itaituba, Pará State, including the employment of minors as prostitutes in mining encampments. In 1988 he was shot dead.

According to interviews conducted by the Pará State Industry Secretariat in 17 mining encampments in the municipality of Itaituba in 1990, young women and girls are enticed to mining camps with promises of high wages in canteens and restaurants. When they reach the mining settlements they find they are to work as prostitutes, to pay off transport and other debts incurred, including medicines to treat malaria. In addition women and girls often have to pay off their own 'price' charged to the brothel owner by the intermediary, who has effectively sold them on.

'The brothels's debt (the transport costs) I paid off quickly, but now I have to pay off my own price ... She (the brothel owner) paid the (intermediary) and now I have to pay her,' explained a 22-year-old prostitute from Maranhão working in one of the mining encampments in Itaituba, Pará in May 1990.

Money for sexual services is paid directly by the mining workers to the brothel owners who hold the money against the women's debts. Since transport costs out of the area are high, and the prostitutes rarely have access to money they have earned, their freedom to leave is curtailed. Women also reported being physically coerced and confined to the brothels, and complained of 'ill-treatment, beatings and imprisonment', and that those trying to escape were killed or tortured. They also alleged that local police connived in holding them in these conditions, arresting and ill-treating those who tried to complain publicly.

National attention was drawn to this question by a series of articles on child prostitution in the north and north-east of Brazil published in the *Folha de São Paulo* in February 1992. Following a public outcry, federal police raided a number of brothels in the mining town of Cuiu-Cuiu, Itaituba, Para and released some 74 prostitutes, many if them minors, and arrested ten brothel owners. Had the raid occurred during the season when mining activity is highest, the number of prostitutes and brothel owners encountered is likely to have been much higher.

Some of the girls, as young as 15, explained to journalists after their release that they had been duped, believing they would work in restaurants, and had been forced into prostitution. They said that one of the girls who tried to resist had been beaten with a chair. While other women released stated that they considered themselves prostitutes, had known they would be working as such in the mining camps, and were willing to return to this activity in other locations, one of their spokeswomen told the press, 'No-one imagined they would become slaves'.

Father Bruno Sechi, Amazonian Co-ordinator of the Street Boys and Girls Movement, said of the police action: *The problem of prostitution of children and adolescents is not confined to this or that mining camp or town. We have evidence to suggest that it occurs throughout Amazonia and is deeply linked to other systems of exploitation and family disintegration in the region. It is vital to carry out a large-scale investigation, to have firmness of purpose and measures to curb this criminal activity which already relies on networks for the abduction, transport and enslavement of girls.*

Brazil has ratified several relevant conventions such as the Convention on the Rights of the Child, the 1956 Supplementary Convention on the Abolition of Slavery, the Slave Trade and Institutions and Practices Similar to Slavery, as well as the Convention for the Suppression of the Traffic in Persons and of the Exploitation of the Prostitution of Others.

Anti-Slavery International urges the Working Group on Contemporary Forms of Slavery of Children to draw attention to this matter and to work with the Brazilian government to seek ways of combating traffic in women and girls.

A women's section in a police station in Brazil. In some Brazilian cities, special sections for women have been set up within police stations, where women who have suffered violence or abuse can receive sympathetic advice. JENNY MATTHEWS/OXFAM

Colombian women prisoners in Britain

Jo Fisher

In 1988, Marta was sentenced to nine years in prison for importing 400 grammes of cocaine into Britain. She is one of 31 Latin American women, the majority Colombians, serving between four and 14 years in British jails for drug smuggling. Like Marta, many feel they passed through the courts simply as 'another Colombian' with little effort made to determine the individual circumstances of their cases. The majority had lawyers who spoke no Spanish at all, only rarely were reports into their backgrounds produced at their trials, and fear of reprisals prevented many women from speaking out in their own defence.

The stories of these Colombian women are closely tied up with their roles as mothers and wives in a society torn apart by violence and where one quarter of the population live in absolute poverty. They show the daily reality of life behind the newspaper reports of atrocities committed by warring cocaine barons, mafia hit-squads and contract-killers in a country notorious as one of the most violent in the world. For the majority of Colombian women in British jails, it was poverty, ignorance and fear which drove them, wittingly or unwittingly, into the cocaine trade.

According to Susana, who was 26 when her husband left his job as a clothes salesman to work as a local drugs courier,

her story is not untypical.

I knew what he was doing, but I was happy because we had enough to pay for the children's clothes, the rent and food, whereas before we always had money problems. The more involved he got, the more money he made. In the end we had a big house, cars, shops and a restaurant. When they get money, men go crazy. They think money is everything and they act like they are God. This is why I did not want him to get involved with the mafia. He used to fix up 'shows' for his friends with prostitutes and cocaine and he gambled. He spent a fortune. I knew all this was going on because I signed all the cheques. I managed all the money but I was not allowed to spend any on myself. He always made it look as if I was controlling every-thing. He could not spend anything and I was totally under his control. I was terrified of him. He was very violent. He beat me badly. I would stand between him and the children and he would beat the three of us senseless.

I think he had always planned to use me. He knew I was a very hard worker and that I would keep the business running while he was out spending. If the police came he could say the business was mine, I would get the blame and he would look like the law-abiding, honest one. I was very young when I fell in love with him and it was only much later that I realised it was not true love, because when he was killed, I felt relief, like a load had been lifted from me. I always though that without him, I would not be able to support my children. I thought that for better or worse, there was always food, money for their education, a roof over our heads, even if the price was his violence. The most important thing to me was my children.

The mafia also saw how degenerate he had become and they got rid of him. We lost everything. We had a lot of debts, so he began to start working again. He went to Peru, carrying drugs. He was caught and put in prison and I went to look after him for a few months. He had been badly tortured and the other prisoners were praying for him, expecting him to die. I had to find the money for a doctor and a lawyer and take him in medicine and food, while my children were with a relative in Columbia. After 18 months he was released.

In prison he made international connections that he never had before. This is the reason why I say prison is never good. When he got out he began to work with a man he had met there, buying and carrying drugs. He returned from a trip one Friday and the following Monday morning they killed him.

I watched him from the window talking to a friend and then the skarios (hired killers) pushed him into a car. They cracked his chest with a rifle, burnt him with cigarettes and in a country lane they broke his spine. When I saw him in the morgue his face was all swollen and his chest and his back was completely black with bruises. Then they finished him off with six shots and left him at the edge of the road.

I did not have a penny. My husband had invested everything we had in the business. I rang his partner to say I needed money for the funeral and to live on. He gave me money. But while I was at the funeral someone went into my flat and

took everything. When I got back only the beds were left. Then the police called me to got to the station to identify a man they caught running away from the scene of the murder. It was the friend I had seen him talking to. Now he knew I had seen him and this caused problems for me. Danger. When I got back to the house there was a car waiting with skarios to kill me. The police protected me and took me and the children away.

Eight days later the partner came and said that my husband owed him eight million pesos and that I had to pay up. I said, 'How am I going to pay it? I have nowhere to live, nothing for my children, absolutely nothing.' He said there was no problem because he had a plan. 'You will work to repay the debt.' I had no choice. If I did not work we would all have been killed. I could not risk the lives of my children. That is how I began carrying drugs.

Once you get involved, they do not let you get out in case you grass on them. Of course you are afraid, but you get used to it, like you get used to being beaten every day. It becomes a way of life.

Most of the Latin American women serving sentences in British jails turned to drug smuggling as a desperate attempt to escape poverty. More than one quarter of households in Colombia's towns and cities are headed by women, social security is practically non-existent, public health provision is limited and work opportunities have been severely hit by the economic crisis. Poor, inexperienced women are easy prey for the drug dealers, who appear to offer quick and easy solutions to their problems. For the safe delivery to Europe of an average of 500-700 grammes of cocaine, usually carried in their stomachs in small packages sealed in condoms or the fingers of surgical gloves, drug couriers can expect to earn several thousand US dollars. They are not told of the fatal consequences if the cocaine packages burst in the stomach, nor of the risk of arrest. Most are told that the worst that can happen to them is that they will be sent back to Colombia on the next flight.

Cristina was in her mid-thirties when she was arrested at Heathrow airport with 500 grammes of cocaine inside her stomach.

My daughter is nine years old and needs an operation to restore her sight. Without it she will almost certainly go blind. We are poor and we could not pay the operation and when someone offered me money to travel abroad, I felt I had no choice but to accept. I was told that I would have to take some medicine to Italy for someone who had become ill. I knew it was prohibited to take it out of the country, but I believed its sale was not illegal in Europe. I brought it in my stomach and to be able to swallow it I had to be injected with something. The customs detained me at the airport, but until that moment I did not really know what a 'bad' drug was.

Since my arrest I have always told the truth. I told the court exactly what made me commit the crime, that I only wanted to cure the sight of my daughter, which is something any desperate mother who loves her children would do. The judge hurt and humiliated me, saying that in sentencing me he would take into account the extenuating circumstances, even though I was probably lying. He sentenced me to eight years.

My 18-year-old son wanders the streets. I don't know what's happening to my daughter. She is with her father, and this is a danger for her, for reasons of a personal nature.

While many judges recognise that women such as these are dispensable to the drug barons, and that lack of information about the tough European penalties for smuggling ensures that couriers will be easily replaced, long sentences are still considered to be a deterrent.

Like all foreign prisoners in British prisons, Colombian women cannot expect early parole and will, on average, serve almost two-thirds of their sentences. The distance from home, and language problems, mean the women suffer loneliness and isolation, many have no one to visit them and no one to talk to. Long prison sentences also spell disaster for the women's families.

Marta has served three-and-a-half years of her nine-year sentence. She carried 400 grammes of cocaine in her stomach, unaware that she was two months pregnant. Her daughter was taken from her when she was one year old and for the past two years Marta has seen her only once a week on prison visits.

The judge said he would be lenient because I was pregnant and he gave me nine years. Being Colombian is enough to give you a long sentence. But they do not understand the situation. When you do not give names, the judges think you do not want to co-operate. They do not understand that you are not protecting the guilty, you are protecting your children.

My children were 17, 18 and ten when I was arrested. They were left alone because I am head of the family. It is the same for all of us. You worry all the time, that they have not got food, that they are sick, that they are getting involved in drugs.

As long as there is a demand for cocaine in the US and Europe, and as long as there is fear and poverty and ignorance in Latin America, the dealers will always find women to carry their drugs. Putting us in prison for years and years isn't going to change that.

Note

For their protection, the names of the women have been changed.

Jo Fisher is the author of two books on Latin America. Her first, *Mothers of the Disappeared*, published in 1989, is about the human-rights struggle in Argentina. Her second book, *Out of the Shadows: Women, Resistance and Politics in South America*, tells the story of women's fight against the generals in Chile, Argentina, Uruguay and Paraguay.

INTERVIEW

Sochua Mu Leiper, Director of Khemara

Now that the peace agreement for Cambodia has been signed, and aid embargoes are beginning to be lifted, foreign agencies are falling over themselves to offer assistance to that beleaguered country. Just a matter of weeks ago, however, the very first local indigenous Cambodian agency was launched, which aims to work exclusively with women. Its director, Sochua Mu Leiper, interviewed in her busy offices in Phnom Penh, talked about the work of Khemara.

What are the particular problems that are facing women in Cambodia?

I think the most difficult problems that Cambodian women are facing these days are first of all the sudden changes in their roles. They used to be just caretakers of their children and now they have to be caretakers, breadwinners, and the core support of the entire family. She has to do that without the help of a husband because during the Pol Pot years, between 1975 and 1979, half of the population — over 2 million Khmer people — died. Nowadays 60 per cent of our population are women, and of that, 30 per cent are widows. In the old days Khmer women were not educated. Even now they are not educated. They lack economic support, educational background, and the emotional and psychological support from partners.

The second problem is the breakdown of the community system. Under the Pol Pot regime, people were moved from one place to the other, because the regime was afraid of people having too much power within a community. They killed people, they moved members of families to different parts of the country, they asked children to spy on their parents, they killed anybody who could read or write, anybody who had any kind of leadership.

The third problem is the total breakdown of the family system. It will be a difficult task for Cambodia in the future to rebuild the community because of the destruction during the four Pol Pot years.

How can Khemara help?

Khemara can help in a very, very small way, but at least we are starting, and we are the first local, indigenous organisation helping our people. We can help by looking at the problems of women as a whole and the family as a whole. We do not want to address just one issue. For example, we will not just look at income generation, or at child-care, or at literacy, we will have an integrated approach. We will have these three services in each project that we design and we will very much promote community participation. We want to empower women, but they need the skills, they need the tools.

Learning to weave, at a Khemara workshop. Khemara

What sort of tools are they? How do you go about building up that sense of trust and community in people who have lost it?

First of all they need to trust themselves, they need to come together, and function together as a group. The trust that was lost has to be built up. For example, when we were training our staff, it was clear that even among our staff members the women do not have trust among themselves, because during the genocide years they were taught not to trust, and in the past ten years life has been so difficult that one lives only for oneself. When I ask people 'do you know your neighbours?' they answer, 'No, we do not have the time to know our neighbours.' So we want to build up trust, otherwise we could not do a community development programme.

After that we will have to give the women responsibility, and not just talk about their needs but really make it possible for them to do something themselves. They have to design the projects, and come up with strategies, even very simple ones, as to who will take care of the children, whose turn is it, how much

money should we contribute, what is the interest rate for the loans, when can you come to the literacy class. Those tasks will be put in the hands of the participants of the projects.

There are lots of NGOs now in Cambodia — there's a new one starting almost every week. Khemara is the first indigenous NGO. Are there problems that Khemara can tackle, which foreign NGOs would not be able to address quite so easily?

As a goal we want to work with the Women's Association in the municipalities — in fact we are already doing it. The Women's Association plays the role of a welfare department but since they do not have the budget from the government they are pretty much under the control of the local authorities, and not really addressing or responding to the needs of the people. They have very many representatives, and a very good organisation, but they do not have the resources. But we have the means, and we will work closely with them. We will train members of the Women's Association together with our staff. We believe that our contribution in the training is very valuable because we take into consideration the values of Cambodian society, the Cambodian family, the community. Those are the things that a local NGO like us can do for the nation.

Do you think there is a value in having all Cambodians as staff? Will they be able to empathise more closely with the people they are working with?

Yes. We selected our staff in a very special way. We selected former members of the Women's Association because they have worked closely with the community for the past 12 years. We selected only women, and one of the criteria for selection was the attitude of the person towards community, the disadvantaged, the handicapped, the poor. It is our principle to say that we will not *serve* the poor, we will *work with* the poor. The other criterion was that the staff member has to have gone through the Pol Pot regime. I think development in Cambodia will face problems at first, because of too much aid coming in at the same time — international aid organisations with expatriate staff wanting to 'save' this nation too fast, without local input. I think that will be the danger for Cambodia.

The fear of a kind of a take-over — is that what you mean?

I fear a take-over, yes. I think in the first five years it will be that way. People coming from outside being so willing to help, people from inside having gone through so much. We are so tired that we want nothing else but assistance, and I fear that the two sides do not communicate.

Khemara is a women's organisation, run by women, for women. Has that been a problem? What do Khmer men feel about it, and what is the attitude of the public?

As far as the organisation is concerned, we almost have the blessing of the government and the community — I have felt so much confidence and so much support from the community. But when it comes to reality, I have had to stand up and stress our goals to men; they are afraid that we will be pampering the women, and that we will take over without preparing the women. Also they are afraid that we might go too fast, because Cambodian society is run by men, even though they are the minority.

We have to tell the public, mainly men, about what we are doing — and that we are not going to take over. The reality is that women have to take care of themselves and women are the roots of this society.

So where will you start? There are so many areas that you could work in, how have you prioritised?

We have given first priority to training. We will be training our staff for nine months in community development. The strength of our staff is that they have gone through the difficult years with the people that they will be working with. But it can also be a weakness. Because they have suffered with them, they do not see that all their pain can be changed, can be challenged. So, for example, if a woman is beating her child, why is it an issue? If she is under stress, she beats her child. So in the training, we ask that question, why is it an issue? How would you respond to this situation?

Secondly, in community development we want to stress that women need to be organised. We really want to emphasise participation of women in the project, and not just *serving* them. Because in the old days, this type of work was done as charity work. Community development did not exist and still does not exist. We will spend three months learning how to do a survey. The staff will design the questionnaire and collect and analyse the data. We really need to know, to have the data, to analyse

Creche at a Khemara project. Khemara

it, to sit down with the community, and say, what is it that you want us to do?

The Peace agreement has been signed now in Paris. What do you think the future is going to be like? Does the future look bright? How optimistic are you?

Well, I have to have some hope, you know! But I see that it is going to be a very, very long, difficult fight. Peace is on paper right now. What does it really mean? We do not know. I think there will be some chaos, because you are dealing with four different groups and you have to face the Khmer Rouge coming back; you are dealing with the political leaders who have been away from the country for 10-20 years. I have worked with them on the border where the refugees are and where the resistance group have control; they have no idea what the country inside is like or what people inside are facing nowadays. There is a great deal of misinformation in the resistance areas and I fear that the people who have gone away for so long have lost touch with the reality in Cambodia.

Secondly, the Khmer Rouge is coming back. People really do not feel right about that. They know that the Khmer Rouge have not changed. I think the government knows but the government wants to stop this war that has gone on for too long. I think in that sense it is right. But I hope that international communities and other countries realise that the government almost had to say yes to signing the Peace Agreement and that they will still have to face the Khmer Rouge. The Khmer Rouge will not let their people come out of their zones.

You know, Cambodia has gone through so much. The country economically is totally destroyed, physically we lack so many resources, and then the people are very tired. They need to have some kind of hope. So in the beginning of the reconstruction years it will be very hard. As I say, I have hopes, but it is difficult, because we have to rebuild from almost nothing, from scratch. It will take another generation of Cambodians to put the country back on its feet.

For example, the children of this generation — what have they seen, what have they witnessed in the past 10-20 years? Nothing but war and instability in their lives. The people who lived in the refugee camps have been away for so long and their children were born in the refugee camps. Now they are coming back, to uncertainty, to their homes that have been destroyed, they are coming back with the refugee mentality. For over ten years they lived in the camps where the UN took care of their needs. Now they are returning to a country that has to start from zero — building your own house, ploughing your own fields — a country that lacks even basic things like clean water, electricity, education for children and women.

So if you had a message for the international community, what would it be?

I would say, let us come out of it slowly. Yes, we need assistance; yes, the children need to go to school; yes, the women need to have a better life. But it has to come out of the context of this society. Giving too much too fast can only destroy the society, and already we see so much of that. Within the past two years since I came back, people talk in terms of dollars even in the countryside. In the capital, you see foreign developers coming in looking at the resources that are still available in Cambodia, coming to take advantage of what is left.

Neighbouring countries will take advantage of Cambodia; and that is very ironic, because during the difficult years, they said, 'No, we do not want to handle the Cambodia problem.' And now that Cambodia is open, they say, 'Oh!, now, Cambodia has problems, we should come and take care of Cambodia.'

Letters to the Editor

The Editor welcomes correspondence from readers in response to articles published in Focus on Gender. We would like the Letters Page to be a place where the views and experiences of readers can be shared. General comments on the journal are also welcome. If you write to the Editor, please indicate whether or not your comments are intended for publication, and please give your full postal address. The Editor reserves the right to abbreviate letters published in this section.

Here are two contrasting responses to the first issue of Focus:

Congratulations to GADU — for your lovely publications on gender and development! Thank you for the copy of *Focus on Gender*. I was very thrilled and I have read each and every page of my copy and I think it's wonderful; the new format is very appealing indeed! I always look forward to reading your publications and I always get a feeling that GADU is ever so vibrant and lively!

It is a reminder of the importance of linking women's projects, as we all have so much to learn and share. I feel quite in a celebrating mood as I write to you.

Nawina Hamaundu
Oxfam Office
Lusaka, Zambia

I hope you will be able to publish all or part of the following letter, for which I recommend the title 'Gender blurred'.

How disappointing to discover that the *Focus on Gender* doesn't apparently intend to focus on gender at all, but on women. I should have spotted this in the journal's subtitle, which, like the rest of the journal, focuses on women rather than on gender issues. A glance down the contents page shows that women writers, writing mainly about women, outnumber men 15:1; the first two pages of Geraldine Reardon's Editorial set the tone with 28 mentions of women and not a single mention of men.

I commend the efforts of the 'Women in Development' movement to offset male bias by enhancing the visibility and participation of women in planned social change. But do the editors and contributors really believe that we can solve gender asymmetries by simply substituting one kind of gender bias for another? It is nothing short of scandalous that a new journal which claims to concern itself with gender issues should be written almost entirely by women and about women, with men censored from the picture except as blurry, threatening background figures. All this creates the unfortunate impression that 'gender issues' are only the concern of women and that they are concerned with women rather than men. I sincerely hope that future editions of the journal will treat us to something more substantial than the sound of one hand clapping.

Dr Neil Thin
Department of Social Anthropology,
The University of Edinburgh,
Adam Ferguson Building, George Square,
Edinburgh, EH8 9LL, UK

News from GADU

1994 UN Meeting on human rights: the women's lobby

Women's rights as human rights is the rallying call of the women's lobby in the build-up to the Vienna UN Conference on Human Rights in June 1994. This will be only the second conference on the subject convened by the UN, and a great deal has happened during the 25 years since the first one took place. As the UN's role as perceived guardian of democracy and peace within the new world order expands, the 1994 Conference must recognise the ways in which women's rights are systematically violated, and the need to integrate them into the concepts, mechanisms and institutions of the UN system.

GADU Coordinator Eugenia Piza-Lopez attended meetings in February 1993 in Costa Rica with members of the Latin America Steering Committee, and DAWN (Development Alternatives for Women for a New Era) groups on development and reproductive rights. She was briefed on the different UN processes and their outcomes, and the role of international NGOs in supporting initiatives promoted by women's networks, as well as the key issues for defining human rights from a gender perspective.

Lobbying around the conference

- For the Latin America/Caribbean satellite meeting 'La nuestra', women organised platforms of black, indigenous, prisoners, and disabled interest groups to gain a broader understanding of the issues. A total of 19 recommendations were put forward and 37 women's organisations and networks gained consultative status at regional level.

- Asia is about to have their regional conference with a high level of participation by women's networks and groups. A three-day NGO meeting, on Women's Rights, Human Rights and the Right to Development in Bangkok last summer had a single coherent focus on 'The Right to be A Woman', and children and minorities were also high on the agenda.

- The recommendations of the Africa regional meeting in Tunisia held last November include a demand to recognise violence against women as a violation of human rights.

- The International Women's Tribune Center and the Center for Women's Global Leadership in the US are organising a series of international hearings on the violation of women's human rights, to inform the UN Commission on Human Rights and the April Preparatory Committee.

- Fringe activities for the Conference include a world tribunal to feed documentation on women's rights violations to the UN Commission. This will be an extremely important event, setting a precedent and providing the first tools for monitoring abuses and violations of women's rights, and integrating new definitions from a gender perspective of what constitute human rights. There will also be nine regional panels and a permanent open-ended short-wave radio station to follow the NGO and the UN meeting.

- In Europe: two Oxfam staff attended the General Assembly of Women in Development Europe (WIDE) in Madrid in February, on the theme of women's rights. Speakers from Zimbabwe, Philippines, Mexico, Tunisia, Nigeria/UK and Croatia raised many serious issues, including the human-rights implications of growing conflict and migration in Europe. Although current human-rights activities fail to consider women's rights, the UN's international instruments still provide a useful framework for analysis. As in previous WIDE assemblies, North and South were challenged on the need to find a common language and strategy. Workshops were held on reproductive rights, economic rights, ethnic conflict and racism in Europe. A full report of the WIDE meeting will be available in April 1993.

Women's International League for Peace and Freedom

WILPF has been lobbying, campaigning and networking for peace and justice in the context of poverty, exploitation, violence, and discrimination since 1915. It is still alive and kicking today – not bad going after nearly 80 years! It has branches in many countries of the world, and an international coordination office in Geneva. Recently members have been involved in linking with women's groups in former Yugoslavia. Here are details of two UK initiatives just launched.

The clothes line has special relevance to this issue's focus on conflict. It aims to produce t–shirts made by survivors of violence, or friends of women victims. WILPF hope that community women's groups will organise local shirt–making sessions and displays of the Clothes line. The variety of designs on display will show that violence against women can take many forms, can help break the silence surrounding gender violence, assist the healing process for those who have suffered, and act as a focus to bring about an end to violence against women. The t–shirts will be brought together in November around the International Day to End Violence Against Women. A similar project in the US was felt to be very successful as a focus for awareness–raising and solidarity.

Community report cards: WILPF are hoping for a strong women's perspective on environment and development at the 1994 Global Forum in Manchester, UK. Based on the healthy planet report cards developed by WEDO (Women's Environment and Development Organisation) they have developed a paper (more environmentally friendly!) version which they hope will be useful for groups auditing their natural, political, and social environment at local level. Social concerns might be such things as the number of people living below the poverty line, levels of violence against women and minorities, or access to equal–opportunity employment.

We wish WILPF every success with these creative ventures! Their international secretariat is based at 1, Rue de Varembe, CP28, 1211 Geneva 20, Switzerland.

New opportunities for funding

EC Budget Lines B7-5051 and B7 5052: Role of women in development: Opportunities for funding of awareness-raising activities about gender are currently available through the European Community in

Brussels, Belgium. The funds will be used primarily within the European Commission to make project officers more aware of women in development issues, and to help set up WID Units in the ministries of developing countries. Research, publications, seminars which contribute to better integration of women's role in policies, would be eligible for grants, and NGOS can apply. The line does not finance activities in the field. For more information, contact Mrs E. Hernandez, DGI, Tel: 299 0739, Building Science 14 (Asia, Latin America and the Mediterranean), or Ms Chapman, tel: 295 0030, Building Evere Green (African, Caribbean and Pacific DCs).

World University Service scheme: Under a scheme operated by WUS, money is available until June 1993 to pay for African nationals to receive training in the North. Women are preferred, working in the field with a senior role in their organisation. Please apply as soon as possible to Nick Alcock, Training Department, Oxfam, 274 Banbury Road, Oxford OX2 7DZ.

INTRAC (International NGO Training Centre:) There are still places available on INTRAC courses, including management strategies, appraisal of development agencies and programmes, and improving the effectiveness of Northern NGOS and Southern partners. The courses, which are aimed at programme and project managers, last three to five days, and take place in the North, including some in Oxford. More information is available from INTRAC, PO Box 563, Oxford OX2 6RZ, UK, tel/fax (44) 0865 201851/2.

Tolerance and respect for diversity and difference
The strength of the triennial International Interdisciplinary Congress on Women lies in the opportunity it offers for the sharing of experiences from diverse points of view. It brings together scholars and practit-

ioners from a wide range of disciplines to share insights and the results of research and to explore issues of importance to women throughout the world.

Previous venues have included universities in Israel, Netherlands and Ireland: 2000 women attended the fifth Congress in February this year in Costa Rica. The success of the Congress is its diversity: 800 papers were presented bringing together feminist research and gender and development issues from many countries in a range of areas — literature, violence against women, sexuality, disability, psychology, and religion. Papers ranged from the very specialised (gender roles and homicides in British Columbia 1920-1923) to the very broad (gender training and development planning).

At this Congress black women's perspectives were of great significance, and a panel discussion focusing on cultural identity raised the issue of similarities within diversity: black and white women must define their own struggle in their own terms. Black Caribbean women's identity, for example, is forged by slavery and myths of the exuberance of slave women, whereas white women's sexuality is conditioned by their protected status and domestication.

A discussion panel of indigenous women from Mexico, Costa Rica, Guatemala, and Belize highlighted the need for indigenous women to find their own identity, linking feminism with sustainable livelihoods and land rights. Indigenous women see their identity as closely related to their physical environment, and their perspective on reproductive rights emphasises the importance of having many children because of the threat of extermination for many indigenous peoples.

One of the interesting aspects of this Congress was its departure from the usual format of individual speakers to include discussion sessions presented by panels, which encouraged networking and enabled issues raised by black women to be transmitted to the academic mainstream. Its weakness was a lack of papers on popular social movements, which emphasised the divide between activists and academics, and may indicate an absence of research on these issues.

Eugenia Piza-Lopez of GADU attended the Congress, giving a paper entitled 'Towards a new dimension of North-South cooperation', on the role of development agencies in the new world order, and how the development paradigm put forward by Southern women can be effectively integrated into the agenda of Northern agencies. On the social side, the Congress offered a huge activities programme, which included exhibitions, sports activities, cinema and dance. The sixth Interdisciplinary Congress will be held in three years' time in Australia.

Crisis has become normality

The Oxfam AGRA (Action for Gender Relations in Asia) meeting in Thailand in February 1993 was entitled 'Development in conflict situations: the gender dimension'. It was attended by representatives from Community Aid Abroad, Oxfam UK and Ireland, Oxfam Hong Kong, Burmese Relief Centre, and ACORD, who provided a facilitator, and Oxfam representatives from East, South and West Asia attended, as well as representatives from the Gender and the Emergencies Units based in Oxford. Case studies were presented examining in depth the effects of conflict on different countries, including Lebanon, Burma, Somalia and Uganda, and on the programmes of development agencies such as Oxfam.

The workshop report questions the assumption that emergency crises are a momentary blip in an otherwise regular progression towards the goal of long-term development. It calls for a new model of development which recognises that emer-

gency interventions must serve the long-term development goals of strengthening the community's own capacity for dealing with rapid and turbulent change. Agencies must take responsibility for deepening their understanding of what happens to communities in conflict, and for developing more sensitive means of communicating with the people they aim to help.

The workshop report looks at how conflicts develop, their impact on gender relations, coping with conflict and trauma, assessing gender needs in conflict situations, the nature of empowerment and disempowerment, and the response of Oxfam's partners to conflict. It is very useful as an analysis of an area of gender and development which up to now has been rather neglected.

How do we discover our gender?

How do we know what it means to be female or male? How do we know when we are grown up? Is it the same when girls become women as when boys become men? What influences our decisions? Is 'growing up' the same all over the world?

Leeds Development Education Centre, UK, has recently established a gender and development project to reflect the experience of young people in Europe, Africa, Asia and South America. This exciting new initiative seeks a global perspective on these and a range of other gender issues. It will produce interactive teaching materials for use with young people aged 9-14, and hopes to support teachers and students in their exploration of the issues surrounding the concepts of gender and development. For more details, contact Chrys Ritson, coordinator of the project at Leeds DEC, 151-153 Cardigan Road, Leeds LS6 1LJ, UK, who hopes to work with gender and development workers and field staff to draw on a wide range of perspectives.

Women-in-development perspectives and practices of the European Commission: a progress report

Eurostep, a network of 22 NGOs from 15 European countries working for justice and equal opportunities for people North and South, is currently lobbying hard to persuade the EC to give a higher profile to its women-in- development (WID) work.

Progress on implementation of the EC's gender policy has been slow. Although the EC Council of Ministers took a decision to integrate gender into EC development policy in 1982, there has been some resistance from implementors and project officers, and WID officers were not appointed until recently (funded by the Netherlands and Danish governments rather than from the EC).

In preparation for a meeting of the EC Development Committee in May when a review of the implementation of WID policies will be on the agenda, members of the Eurostep gender group have just drawn up an evaluation of the EC's gender policy to be circulated to EC ministers responsible for development cooperation. It recommends:

- staffing of the WID Desks of DGI (Directorate General I, dealing with External Affairs) and DG VIII (Development and Cooperation) with 2 WID coordination posts, supplemented by WID experts on long-term contracts, and gender specialists on the staff of the five technical divisions;
- gender training should be provided for all EC staff who deal with project planning and implementation;
- EC delegations appraising projects should establish regular contacts with women's organisations and national bodies with gender competence;
- gender criteria should always be taken into consideration before approval of projects, supplemented by gender-specific target analyses to enable better understanding of the different activities of men and women.

Workshop at the AGRA meeting in Thailand.   Oxfam

Resources

Book review

Out of the Shadows documents the growth of grassroots women's organisations in the countries of the Southern Cone of Latin America. It illustrates how women emerged into the public arena in reaction to the economic and political excesses of the military dictatorships and to demand an end to human-rights violations. It also examines what the recent return to democracy in the Southern Cone has meant to the lives of women who are among the most socially marginalised.

Until the 1970s Argentina, Chile and Uruguay had enjoyed a higher level of development than most other countries in Latin America, which meant better health care, education and economic development, but all this was lost following the military coups. The regimes' economic and political programmes provoked the surge in women's public participation, as falling living standards, growth in unemployment, chronic poverty, and cuts in state welfare forced women to look for communal solutions in order to feed their families.

There are few publications about the lives of people in Paraguay, even fewer about women's organisations. The book provides us with an insight into the harsh reality for Paraguayans who lived under a dictator-ship for 34 years. There are

common patterns in all four countries, illustrated by the way in which women became aware of their oppression and began to organise in the face of the reign of terror unleashed by brutal dictatorships. The women's lives were also affected by an ideological offensive which called for a return to traditional values, and proclaimed that women's place was in the home. Ironically it was their roles as wives and mothers and their concern for the welfare of their families which drove women into the public domain.

Jo Fisher shows how grassroots organisations represent a potential for transforming women's lives and revitalising working class organisation. She describes the form 'popular' participation takes, the variety of women's organisations, and their role in the workplace. For example, the Union of Housewives in Argentina has raised housework as an issue with trade unions. In Uruguay, women trade unionists have challenged traditional practices, and introduced gender issues into political life, with the result that changes are slowly taking place in the private sphere.

This book does not offer any general prescriptions nor suggest how to ease the immense burdens shouldered by working class and peasant women in developing countries. But it does portray women's self-reliance, giving us an insight into their lives, the hardships they confront, and in particular, the constraints that women face to participation in activities to bring about changes in their situation.

The book makes it clear that a return to democratic government does not mean immediate benefits for all women. Public spending cuts imposed by structural-adjustment measures mean that poverty is a major reason for women organising. Self-help and communal responses are still essential for survival in shanty towns, and women need support to organise at a strategic level in order to make their demands known to decision makers. The benefits of democracy are not automatic, and development aid to support these initiatives therefore continues to be a priority.

This book is very readable and should be of interest to the non-specialist. Much of the information in the book was gathered by extensive interviewing, and the book gives a voice to women whose experiences are usually left out of the analysis. In their own words, they tell us of the impact of repression and debt crisis on their lives.

Jo Fisher sensitively explores the diversity of interests of women from different social backgrounds. In Chile (where there is a growth in grassroots feminism) domestic violence, sexuality, education, and childcare have become issues for some organisations, but others are deeply suspicious of feminist ideas. Flora, one of the women interviewed, feels that while all women face gender discrimination, working-class women are confronted with different problems:

We have things in common with middle-class women but we also have other problems they don't have, like the housing shortage, debt problems, unemployment, and we're not going to advance as women if the two aren't closely linked.

While in Paraguay, where peasant women only began to organise for the first time in 1985, the issues are more basic as expressed by Pastora:

Women still work more than men, that hasn't changed. Women still have to work in the house and look after the children and on top of that there's the organisations and the communal work...

One of the biggest obstacles for women organising in strongly 'machista' cultures is male opposition. The slogan picked up by some of the women's organisations — Democracy in the Country and in the Home — clearly expresses the struggle ahead. The book portrays the women's efforts in dealing with male opposition as a gradual process of re-educating partners and colleagues. Jo Fisher points out that women have democratised politics by bringing gender issues into the political parties and trade unions where they are learning to stand up for themselves and the issues that immediately concern them.

The book does not attempt to measure the changes for women in the Southern Cone. But what is very clear is that women have challenged the traditional image of the subservient housewife and developed new relationships with other women based on solidarity and shared experiences. Women have also begun to resist sexism, expressed in different forms in political parties, unions, in the community and the home.

An important message from this book, and a challenge for the women's movement in Britain and around the world, is the need to search for common ground, to respect the diversity of women from different cultures and classes and convert it into a source of strength to challenge cultural values, influence decision makers, and transform development policy.

Marilyn Thomson is a writer, researcher and consultant on gender issues in development.

Out of the Shadows is written by Jo Fisher and published in 1993 by Latin America Bureau, London, UK.
ISBN 0 906156 77 7 (paperback) £7.99.

Further reading

Agarwal, B (ed) (1988) *Structures of Patriarchy: state, community and household in modernising Asia*, New Delhi and London, Kali for Women and Zed Books.

Akhtar, F (1992) *Depopulating Bangladesh: essays on the politics of fertility*, Dhaka, Bangladesh, UBINIG and Narigrantha Prabartana

Amnesty International (1991) *Women in the Front Line: human rights violations against women*, London, Amnesty International.

Amnesty International (1992) *Rape and Sexual Abuse: torture and ill-treatment in detention. An External Paper*, London, Amnesty International.

Anderson, M B and Woodrow, P (1989) *Rising from the Ashes: development strategies in times of disaster*, Boulder and San Francisco, Westview Press.

Ashworth, G (1985) *Of Violence and Violation: women and human rights*, London, Change.

Ashworth, G (1992) 'Women and Human Rights', unpublished paper, London, Change.

Ashworth, G (ed) (forthcoming, November 1993) *A Diplomacy of the Oppressed: new directions in international feminism*, London, Zed Books.

Bunch, C (1991) 'Women's rights as human rights: toward a re-vision of human rights', New York, Center for Women's Global Leadership.

Carrillo, R (1991) 'Violence against women: an obstacle to development', New York, Center for Women's Global Leadership.

Commonwealth Secretariat Women and Development Programme (1992) *Confronting Violence: a manual for Commonwealth action*, London, Commonwealth Secretariat.

Convention on the Rights of the Child was drawn up at the World Summit for Children in 1989 and adopted by the UN General Assembly in 1989 and entered into force on September 2, 1990.

Convention on Elimination of all Forms of Discrimination against Women (CEDAW) was adopted and opened for signature, ratification and accession by the UN General Assembly on December 18, 1979.

Davies, M (ed) (forthcoming 1993) *Women and Violence: a global crisis*, London, Zed Books.

Dawit, S (forthcoming 1994) *Female Genital Mutilation: violence and women's human rights*, London, Zed Books.

DAWN (1991) *Alternatives Volume II: women's visions and movements*, Rio de Janeiro, Development Alternatives with Women in a New Era (DAWN).

Department of Women and Child Development (1991) *The Lesser Child: the girl in India*, Ministry of Human Resource Development, Government of India.

El Bushra, J and Piza-Lopez, E (forthcoming) *Development in Conflict: the gender dimension*, Report of Oxfam meeting in Thailand, February 1993, Oxford, Oxfam.

Elson, D (1991) 'Gender issues in development strategies', paper presented to Seminar on Integration of Women in Development, Vienna, December 9-11.

Ferris, E (1989) 'A world turned upside down' in *Refugees* 70, November.

Fisher, J (1993) *Out of the Shadows: women resistance and politics in South America*, London, Latin American Bureau.

Forbes M S (1992) *Refugee Women*, London, Zed Books.

Forward Looking Strategies for the Advancement of Women (1985) adopted by the World Conference to Review and Appraise the Achievements of the UN Decade for Women.

Hartman, B (1987) *Reproductive Rights and Wrongs: the global politics of population control and contraceptive choice*, New York, Harper and Row.

Henriquez, N and Alfaro R M (eds) (1991) *Mujeres, violencia y derechos humanos*, Madrid, IEPALA.

Hooks, M (1991) *Guatemalan Women Speak*, London, Catholic Institute for International Relations.

Humanistic Committee on Human Rights and Vrouwenberaad Ontwikkelingssamen (1992) *Basta Working Conference 10 December: Reader prepared for conference, Strategies and actions to stop violations of women's human rights*, Amsterdam.

Humanistic Committee on Human Rights and Vrouwenberaad Ontwikkelingssamen (1993) *Basta Working Conference 10 December: Recommendations of the conference, Strategies and actions to stop violations of women's human rights*, Amsterdam.

Inter-Africa Committee on Traditional Practices Affecting the Health of Women and Children (IAC) (1990) *Report of Regional Conference on Traditional Practices Affecting the Health of Women and Children*, Addis Ababa, November 19-24.

Isis WICCE (1990/91) *Poverty and Prostitution, Women's World* 24, Winter.

Jelin, E (ed) (1990) (English translation), *Women and Social Change in Latin America*, London, Zed Books.

Kelkar, G (1987) 'Violence against women: an understanding of responsibility', in Davies, M (ed) *Third World, Second Sex, Volume 2*, London, Zed Books.

Mama, A (1989) *The Hidden Struggle: statutory and voluntary sector responses to violence against black women in the home*, London, London Race and Housing Research Unit.

Marcus, J (1993) *A World of Difference: Islam and gender hierarchy in Turkey*, London, Zed Books.

Mellor, M (1992) *Breaking the Boundaries: towards a feminist green socialism*, London, Virago Press.

Moser, C (1989) 'Gender planning in the Third World: meeting practical and strategic gender needs', *World Development* 17; 11, November.

Mukhopadhyay, M (1990) 'Women's struggle to

512119

save the forest in India in ... in Women in ... Development, Report fro... ... Women's F... Norway, May 14-15, London, IIED.

Ngcobo, L (1989) 'Forced to leave: forced migration of South African women', in *African Woman 3*, Spring.

Papers from the Expert Group Meeting, 1990, on Refugee and Displaced Women and Children, in Vienna, July.

Sachs, W (ed) (1992) *The Development Dictionary: a guide to knowledge as power*, London, Zed Books.

Sancho, N (1989) 'The human rights situation of Filipino women and their response two years after February 1986', in GABRIELA's Commission for Human Rights (1989) *Let's work together for the protection of human rights of Filipino women: a documentation report on the human rights situation of Filipino Women*, Quezon City, GABRIELA.

Sen, A K (1990) 'Gender and cooperative conflicts', in Tinker, I (ed) (1990) *Persistent Inequalities*, Oxford, Oxford University Press.

Spallone, P (1989) *Beyond Conception: the new politics of reproduction*, London, Macmillan.

Sparr, P (ed) (forthcoming, November 1993) *Mortgaging Women's Lives: feminist critiques of structural adjustment*, London, Zed Books.

Taylor, J and Stewart, S (1991) *Sexual and Domestic Violence: help, recovery and action in Zimbabwe*, (a manual for those offering help, support or counselling to women or children who have been sexually assaulted, or to women who suffer violence in their homes), Harare, A von Glehn and J Taylor in collaboration with Women and Law in Southern Africa.

Thomasevski, K (1993) *Women and Human Rights*, London, Zed Books.

Umfreville, M (pseudonym) (1990) *Sexonomycs: an introduction to the political economy of sex, time and gender*, London, Change.

United Nations (1989) *Violence Against Women in the Family*, New York, UN.

United Nations (1991) *The World's Women: trends and statistics 1970-1990*, New York, UN.

Warnock, K (1990) *Land Before Honour: Palestinian women in the Occupied Territories*, London, Macmillan.

Women and Development Europe (WIDE) (1993) *Women, Development and Human Rights*, Report of conference, Madrid, February, 1993, Dublin, WIDE.

Women Working Worldwide (eds) (1991) *Common Interests: women organising in global electronics*, London, Women Working Worldwide.

Zafar, F (ed) (forthcoming, December 1993) *Finding Our Way: women in Pakistan*, London, Zed Books.

PERIODICALS

Agenda. A Journal about Women and Gender, PO Box 37432, Overport, 4067 Durban, South Africa.

African Woman, Quarterly Development Journal of Akina Mama wa Afrika, 4 Wild Court, London WC2.

Anti-Slavery Newsletter, Anti-Slavery International, 180 Brixton Road, London SW9 6AT; also publish an annual *Anti-Slavery Reporter*.

CAFRA News, Caribbean Association of Feminist Research and Action, PO Bag 442, Tunapuna, Trinidad and Tobago.

DAWN Informs, DAWN, c/o Peggy Antrobus, Women and Development Unit, University of the West Indies, Pinelands, St Michael, Barbados.

Flights, Women's Resource and Research Center, UP PO 110, Diliman, Quezon City, The Philippines.

Isis International Women's Journal, Isis International, Casilla 2067, Correo Centrale, Santiago, Chile or 85a East Maya Street, Thilamlife Homes, Quezon City, The Philippines.

Manushi, C1/202 Lajpat Nagar, New Delhi, India.

Minority Rights Group Report, (occasional), 379 Brixton Road, London SW9 7DE.

National Women's Network Newsletter, Box 110, 190 Upper Street, London N1 IRQ.

Peace News, 55 Dawes Street, London SE17 1EL.

Refugees, United Nations High Commissioner for Refugees, PO Box 2500, 1211 Geneva 2 Depot, Switzerland.

The Woman's Watch, Newsletter of International Women's Rights Action Watch (IWRAW), University of Minnesota, 301, 19th Avenue S., Minneapolis, MN 55455, USA.

Update, GABRIELA, PO Box 4386, Manila 2800, The Philippines.

War Resisters International News, 55 Dawes Street, London SE17 1El.

Women Living Under Muslim Law Dossier, BP 23, 34790 Grabels, France.

Women's Global Network for Reproductive Rights Newsletter, Nieuwe Zijds Voorburghwal 32, 1012 RZ Amsterdam, Netherlands.